Documents in Contempo. ...

General editor
Kevin Jefferys
Faculty of Arts and Education, University of Plymouth

Britain in the Second World War

Was the Second World War a great turning-point in British social history? This concise, readable volume provides original documents from the war years which will help the reader evaluate claims that the war introduced a new sense of social solidarity and social idealism which led to a consensus on welfare state reform. It provides important evidence on employment policy, race relations and anti-Semitism, women, health and the family, in addition to examining the Blitz, evacuation and the making of social policy. Special attention is paid to the internal debate within the Conservative Party on the Beveridge Report and the proposed national health service. Many of the documents are drawn from the Public Record Office and have not previously been published.

Harold L. Smith is Professor of History at the University of Houston-Victoria.

Documents in Contemporary History is a series designed for sixth-formers and undergraduates in higher education: it aims to provide both an overview of specialist research on topics in post-1939 British history and a wide-ranging selection of primary source material.

Already published

Alan Booth   *British economic development since 1945*

Stephen Brooke   *Reform and reconstruction: Britain after the war, 1945–51*

Kevin Jefferys   *War and reform: British politics during the Second World War*

Ritchie Ovendale   *British defence policy since 1945*

Scott Lucas   *Britain in Suez: the lion's last roar*

Sean Greenwood   *Britain and European integration since the Second World War*

Forthcoming

Stuart Ball   *The Conservative Party, 1940–92*

John Bayliss   *Anglo-American relations: the rise and fall of the special relationship*

Steven Fielding   *The Labour Party: Socialism and society since 1951*

Rodney Lowe   *The classic welfare state in Britain*

Documents in Contemporary History

Britain in the Second World War

A social history

Edited by

Harold L. Smith

Professor of History, University of Houston-Victoria

Manchester University Press
Manchester and New York
Distributed exclusively in the USA and Canada by St. Martin's Press

Copyright © Harold L. Smith 1996

Published by Manchester University Press
Oxford Road, Manchester M13 9NR, UK
and Room 400, 175 Fifth Avenue, New York, NY 10010, USA

Distributed exclusively in the USA and Canada
by St. Martin's Press, Inc., 175 Fifth Avenue, New York,
NY 10010, USA

British Library Cataloguing-in-Publication Data
A catalogue record for this book is available from the British Library

Library of Congress Cataloging-in-Publication Data applied for

ISBN 0–7190–4492–8 *hardback*
     0–7190–4493–6 *paperback*

First published 1996
00 99 98 97 96   10 9 8 7 6 5 4 3 2 1

Printed by Bell and Bain Ltd, Glasgow

Contents

Acknowledgements

For permission to reproduce copyright material, the publishers and editor should like to thank the following: the Controller of Her Majesty's Stationery Office for Crown copyright material held in the Public Record Office, London (1.3, 1.6, 1.7, 1.10, 1.12, 1.13, 1.16, 2.1–5, 2.7–11, 2.14, 3.1–9, 4.1, 4.3–5, 4.8, 4.10, 4.12, 4.13, 5.1, 5.3–5, 5.7, 6.1–3, 6.8–10, 7.1–5, 8.4–9, 8.11–13, 9.1, 9.2, 9.7, 9.8, 9.11, 10.1, 10.2, 10.4, 10.6, 10.8–13, 10.15, 10.16, 11.1, 11.2, 11.4, 11.7–9, 12.1–3, 12.6); the National Council of Women of Great Britain for the extract from the *Women in Council Newsletter* (1.9); *The Economist* (1.15, 5.12); John Murray (Publishers) Ltd for the extract from Mass-Observation's *People in Production* (2.6); Lord Woolton (2.12, 9.13); the Co-operative Women's Guild for permission to quote the Emergency Resolution on Rationing (2.13); Nigel Nicolson (2.15, 9.4); Joanna Mack and Steve Humphries for the extract from *The Making of Modern London 1939–1945: London at War*, Sidgwick and Jackson, 1985 (2.16); Lord Moyne (3.2); the Fawcett Society (4.1); Elizabeth Roberts for extracts from *Women and Families: An Oral History, 1940–1970*, Blackwell, 1995 (4.14, 5.2); the Curtis Brown Group Ltd for material © of the Trustees of the Mass-Observation Archive at the University of Sussex (5.8); the Married Women's Association (5.9); Joan Allen (5.10); Sage Publications for material from Herman Mannheim, *Annals of the American Academy of Political and Social Science*, vol. 217, September 1941, pp. 134–6 (6.4); the Conservative Party (1.4, 4.15, 9.5, 9.6, 11.6, 12.8); the Labour Party (12.5); the University of Chicago Press (12.7); *The Guardian* © (5.11). Every reasonable effort has been made to contact all copyright holders, and the publishers and editor deeply regret if any have been inadvertently overlooked.

Special thanks are due to David Doughan, Fawcett Library Director, for assistance in obtaining rare material; to Michelle O'Connell, MUP editor, for help in obtaining copyright permissions; and, above all, to my in-house editor and life partner: Judith N. McArthur.

Chronology of events

1939

September   Personal Injuries (Emergency Powers) Act establishes sex-differentiated compensation for civilians injured by enemy action.
First evacuation of mothers and children.

1940

January   Publication of the Barlow Report, *Report of the Royal Commission on the Distribution of the Industrial Population.*

March   Old Age and Widows' Pensions Act reduces women's pensionable age to 60.

May–June   Evacuation of British forces from Dunkirk.

June   National Milk Scheme provides free milk and vitamins for pregnant women and children under five.

July   School meals scheme extended to provide a hot meal for most schoolchildren.

July–September   Battle of Britain.

August   Government decision to retain food subsidies for the duration of the war in an attempt to prevent pressure for wage increases.

1941

December   National Service (No. 2) Act allows the government to conscript women into munitions factories and the women's services.

1942

August   Publication of the Scott Report, *Report of the Committee on Land Utilisation in Rural Areas.*

September   Publication of the Uthwatt Report, *Report of the Committee on Compensation and Betterment.*

November   Defence Regulation 33B allows the government to force a person to undergo examination and treatment for venereal disease if named by two infected persons.

December	Publication of the Beveridge Report, *Social Insurance and Allied Services*.

1943
April	Women civilians granted equal compensation for war injuries.
July	Royal Commission on Population announced.
July	Publication of the white paper *Educational Reconstruction*.
July	Publication of the Norwood Report, *Curriculum and Examinations in Secondary Schools*.

1944
February	Publication of the white paper *A National Health Service*.
March	House of Commons votes to introduce equal pay in teaching but the vote is reversed later because of the government's opposition.
June	Publication of the white paper *Employment Policy*.
June	Publication of the white paper *The Control of Land Use*.
August	Education Act introduces free secondary education.
September	Publication of the white paper *Social Insurance*.
November	Town and Country Planning Act grants local authorities limited powers to rebuild bombed sections of cities.

1945
March	Care of Children Committee (Curtis Committee) appointed.
May	Coalition government replaced by interim Conservative government.
June	Family Allowances Act provides payment of 5s weekly to the mother for each child after the first.
5 July	General election.

Introduction

I

Two questions dominate the debate on the Second World War home front. Did the war create a new sense of social unity which bridged class and other prewar divisions? Did the war produce a consensus on domestic policy which provided the basis for the postwar welfare state and full-employment policy? With the exception of Angus Calder's classic study, *The People's War*, most general accounts of the home front have stressed the themes of social unity and consensus. But research on specific groups and policies has undermined this model by drawing attention to the continuation of prewar social conflicts and to the policy differences dividing the Labour and Conservative parties.

Richard Titmuss established social unity and consensus as central features of the Second World War home front in *Problems of Social Policy*. Titmuss claimed that military defeat at Dunkirk, the Blitz and the threat of invasion in the following months resulted in a dramatic change in people's attitudes and in social policy: 'the mood of the people changed and, in sympathetic response, values changed as well'.[1] From shared danger sprang the conviction that resources should also be shared. Instead of viewing the government's proper role as being limited to assisting the poor, the public became convinced that the government should intervene to ward off distress among all classes: 'damage to homes and injuries to persons were not less likely among the rich than the poor and so ... the assistance provided by the Government ... was offered to all groups in the community'.[2]

---

[1] Richard Titmuss, *Problems of Social Policy*, London, 1950, p. 508.
[2] Titmuss, *Problems of Social Policy*, p. 506.

1

While there is evidence of increased social solidarity in 1940 during the Blitz, it should not be overstated. The notion that a new sense of community emerged as a result of rich and poor sharing public shelters during raids in particular seems exaggerated. The November 1940 London shelter census revealed that only 9 per cent of the population spent the night in public shelters and another 4 per cent in tube stations.[3] It is likely that most middle- and upper-class people were among the vast majority relying on private shelters for protection. Enemy bombs could make the rich as well as the poor homeless, but it is misleading to suggest that all classes suffered equally in this respect during 1940. The working-class areas of London's East End suffered so disproportionately that the Queen admitted to a sense of relief when a bomb finally struck Buckingham Palace.

In focusing on the emergence of a 'Dunkirk spirit', Titmuss paid insufficient attention to behaviour inconsistent with that idea. In June 1940 the government found 'patriotism and peril curiously transient' as substitutes for traditional financial incentives in persuading firms to increase war production.[4] Normally law-abiding citizens were responsible for the increase in looting during 1940 and 1941, not professional criminals. While endorsing rationing in principle, ordinary people circumvented its effects on themselves by black-market purchases. Increased levels of taxation resulted in tax evasion becoming more widespread.[5]

Titmuss and others have portrayed the Second World War as a 'people's war', implying that during the 1940 crisis the class-divided Britain of the 1930s gave way to a united national community in which rich and poor stood shoulder to shoulder against the Germans. This view was originally constructed during the war for patriotic purposes. By mid-1940, Ministry of Information officials had agreed that the 'keynote' of government propaganda should be the idea that it was a 'people's war'.[6] Information which would undermine this view was suppressed, sometimes by the government's censors but often voluntarily by

---

[3] Terence H. O'Brien, *Civil Defence*, London, 1955, p. 508.
[4] Survey by Lord Stamp, June 1940. Cited in W. K. Hancock and M. M. Gowing, *British War Economy*, London, 1975, p. 340.
[5] Paul Addison, *The Road to 1945*, London, 1977, p. 130.
[6] Marion Yass, *This Is Your War: Home Front Propaganda in the Second World War*, London, 1983, p. 28.

the media. The government, for example, refused to allow the BBC to broadcast programmes discussing British anti-Semitism.[7] Seeking to maintain the image of national unity, the BBC voluntarily refrained from mentioning strikes during the war's first four years.[8]

But the government was not alone in promoting the notion of a 'people's war'. Left-wing intellectuals such as J. B. Priestley may have been even more effective in converting the public to the idea. In his 1940 BBC 'Postscript' broadcasts, Priestley used the concept to justify social reform: a 'people's war' must lead to a 'people's peace'. Once the idea had taken root, different groups used it for different purposes. For Conservatives, it was perceived as a form of popular patriotism, creating the national unity which made victory in the war possible. For Labour, it was a powerful image of community, representing a step toward a classless society.

The postwar popularity of the idea of a people's war should not be allowed to obscure the very different ways groups experienced the war. In focusing on social unity, the Titmuss model provides a view of society from the top down, as it appeared to middle- and upper-class observers. It ignores the wartime experience of racial and ethnic minorities, the evidence of increased gender conflict, the social disorganisation implied in the rising crime and juvenile delinquency rates, and the extent to which class feeling remained strong during the war. Studies reflecting the way working-class people viewed the war, such as Tony Lane's account of merchant seamen, do not support the concept of a people's war.[9]

The following chapters provide documents relevant to the debate on social unity and policy consensus. The opening of most of the Public Record Office files relating to the war has contributed to the reassessment of the Titmuss model. On the process of policy making, I have made extensive use of Public Record Office files revealing the debates within the government, previously unpublished material from the archives of the leading political parties, and selections from the diaries and letters of

[7] Tony Kushner, *The Persistence of Prejudice: Antisemitism in British Society during the Second World War*, Manchester, 1989, p. 139.
[8] Justin Davis Smith, 'The struggle for control of the air-waves: the Attlee governments, the BBC and industrial unrest, 1945–51', in Anthony Gorst, L. Johnman and W. S. Lucas (eds), *Post-war Britain, 1945–64*, London, 1989, p. 54.
[9] Tony Lane, *The Merchant Seamen's War*, Manchester, 1990.

political leaders informed about policy formation. I have relied heavily on Home Intelligence reports[10] to convey the public reaction to the government's policy changes. In attempting to convey how Britons experienced the war, I have drawn upon a variety of sources: letters, Mass-Observation reports, news stories, and publications by organisations seeking reform, as well Home Intelligence material.

II

The war created new threats to civilian health and resulted in greater state intervention to protect public health. Civilian death rates rose, and during each year of the war were higher than in 1938. Although prewar government predictions that there would be massive civilian casualties were wildly exaggerated, civilians experienced a higher risk of death from enemy action than in most previous wars. The number of civilians killed by enemy action exceeded that in the armed forces until D-day in 1944. Civilian casualties from enemy action were nearly evenly divided between the sexes: of the 130,000 British civilians who were killed or seriously wounded during the war, 48 per cent were female.

The history of British wartime public health falls into two distinct periods. From 1939 to 1942 the prewar trend toward declining infant mortality, maternal mortality, venereal disease and tuberculosis rates was reversed. Between 1943 and 1945, however, infant, child and maternal mortality rates fell rapidly. By 1945 the infant mortality rate was 20 per cent below the prewar level, while the 1945 maternal mortality rate was almost half what it had been in 1938.

But even in the final years of the war, regional, class, gender and age inequalities in health remained (document 1.14).[11,12]

[10] In March 1940 the Home Intelligence Department was established within the Ministry of Information to survey public opinion on issues of concern to the government. The Home Intelligence reports were compiled using the reports submitted by thirteen regional officers. The latter often quoted individuals whose views seemed to reflect widespread opinion on an issue.

[11] Stillbirth rates fell in all regions during the war, but even at their lowest level, in 1945, the stillbirth rate per 1,000 total births in Wales was 34 compared with 24 in south-east England. Jay Winter, 'Unemployment, nutrition and infant mortality in Britain, 1920–50', in Jay Winter (ed.), *The Working Class in Modern British History*, Cambridge, 1983, p. 239.

[12] Hereafter documents are referred to only by number, e.g. (1.2).

Maternal mortality, for example, still varied considerably by social class: in the immediate postwar period maternal mortality rates for the lowest social stratum were almost 50 per cent higher than the rate for wives belonging to the social elite. Class differences in mortality rates from respiratory tuberculosis among wives were greater immediately following the war than in 1932.[13]

During the 1930s British population trends stimulated alarm about the future, and the war intensified this concern. The long-term fall in the birth rate aroused fears of population decline, of the ageing of the population, and of inadequate numbers of young people for industry and the armed forces. The Beveridge Report strengthened these fears (1.1), and when almost ninety MPs signed a motion expressing alarm at the anticipated population decline, the government in 1943 agreed to an inquiry (1.3). Although the Royal Commission on Population did not report until 1949, its appointment reflected the growing pressure for a positive population policy. This partly explains the introduction of family allowances and other measures to make motherhood more appealing to women; it also helped create a climate of opinion which portrayed motherhood as women's most important role.

The wartime concern with increasing Britain's population growth resulted in increased attention to maternal health. The June 1940 National Milk Scheme made subsidised or free milk available to all pregnant or nursing mothers; by 1943, 70 per cent of those eligible were participating. In 1942 the Vitamin Welfare Scheme was extended to include expectant and nursing mothers (and children under five), allowing them free or inexpensive orange juice, cod liver oil or vitamin A and D tablets.[14] Also, the number of hospital maternity beds rose by 50 per cent during the war, thus ensuring that the prewar trend

---

[13] Michael Anderson, 'The social implications of demographic change', in F. M. L. Thompson (ed.), *The Cambridge Social History of Britain 1750–1950. Vol. 2: People and Their Environment*, Cambridge, 1990, p. 24.

[14] The percentage of those eligible who accepted these services was considerably lower than for the Milk Scheme: orange juice 46 per cent; vitamin tablets 34 per cent; and cod liver oil 21 per cent. Ann Oakley, *The Captured Womb: A History of the Medical Care of Pregnant Women*, Oxford, 1984, p. 124.

towards the hospitalisation of childbirth continued. By the end of the war for the first time a majority of births took place in an institution.[15]

Special efforts were also devoted to improving child health through better nutrition. The evacuation of 826,000 unaccompanied schoolchildren from the larger cities at the beginning of the war disrupted the provision of free meals and milk to needy schoolchildren and forced the government to consider alternatives. Shortly after Dunkirk the government extended from poor to all schoolchildren the prewar milk-in-schools scheme, providing free or subsidised milk, and increased the number who were eligible for free school meals. By 1942, 77.9 per cent of all schoolchildren were receiving school milk.

Titmuss used the milk-in-schools scheme to illustrate his view that evacuation and the Dunkirk spirit stimulated a new social conscience, which found expression in support for universal social services. But the relationship with Dunkirk appears to be chronological rather than causal. The milk-in-schools scheme began in the mid-1930s and planning was already under way to increase distribution before the war broke out. The threat of submarine blockade resulted in the adoption of a national food policy in June 1940 which accelerated acceptance of the milk-in-schools scheme. The shift from providing milk to means-tested poor children to all schoolchildren did not reflect the adoption of a new principle of universality. It was a practical decision forced on policy makers when evacuation dispersed children, making it impossible to keep track of who was eligible for means-tested milk.[16]

The government claimed the nutritional standard of elementary schoolchildren had 'almost certainly' improved during the war. While this was true, it deflects attention from how slowly the improvement occurred. Only 14 per cent of all schoolchildren were receiving school meals by February 1942, and it was not until the war's final year that the proportion rose above one-third.[17]

---

[15] Irvine London, *Death in Childbirth: An International Study of Maternal Care and Maternal Mortality 1800–1950*, Oxford, 1992, p. 265.

[16] John Macnicol, 'The effect of the evacuation of schoolchildren on official attitudes to state intervention', in H. L. Smith (ed.), *War and Social Change: British Society in the Second World War*, Manchester, 1986, pp. 22–4.

[17] D. J. Oddy, 'The health of the people', in Theo Barker and Michael Drake (eds), *Population and Society in Britain*, New York, 1982, p. 133.

Some recipients did not think the programme was implemented effectively. The quality was not always high, and children resisted overcooked food that was unappetising in appearance (1.5).

Especially for lower-income groups, the wartime diet was superior to that before 1939 and contributed to the improved health of the population by 1942. People ate more vegetables, less sugar and fatty meat, and ate dark bread from which less of the vitamin content had been removed by milling.[18] But during the first three years of the war, per capita food consumption fell 18 per cent below the prewar level and was still 10 per cent lower as late as 1944.[19] Energy intake for urban working-class families declined to slightly less than 2,300 kilocalories in 1942, considerably under the 3,400 minimum recommended for the 'average man' by the British Medical Association's Nutrition Committee in the 1930s.[20] This may explain why some manual workers felt they were fatigued from not getting enough to eat (2.9).

Tuberculosis (TB) was an exception to the tendency for civilian health to improve after 1942. The number of new cases of respiratory TB registered rose from 37,879 in 1938 to a peak of 44,664 in 1944 before falling slightly in the war's final year.[21] In September 1943 the government began paying allowances to those in early stages of infection, hoping they would withdraw from employment before infecting other workers (1.15). But non-pulmonary and advanced pulmonary cases were denied allowances in order to limit expenditure. Because of this restriction only about 10 per cent of registered TB patients were covered by the scheme. Also, the free milk provided to school-children was not pasteurised to prevent it from spreading TB.

---

[18] Rising beer and tobacco consumption, however, may have been less beneficial to health. Neither were rationed and, as a consequence, beer consumption rose by 25 per cent during the war, while by 1943 tobacco imports were higher than before the war.
[19] Winter, 'Unemployment, nutrition and infant mortality', p. 250.
[20] D. J. Oddy, 'Food, drink and nutrition', in F. M. L. Thompson (ed.), *The Cambridge Social History of Britain 1750–1950. Vol. 2: People and Their Environment*, Cambridge, 1990, p. 277.
[21] Part of the increase was due to improved diagnosis but there was a real increase in the number of persons with TB during the war. Sheila Ferguson and Hilde Fitzgerald, *Studies in the Social Services*, London, 1954, p. 257.

Before 1939 children under four years had the highest incidence of the form of TB spread by milk consumption, but by the end of the war those aged five to nine had the highest rate.[22]

Before the war, tuberculosis-induced mortality had fallen almost every year from 1920 to 1938. During 1940 and 1941 the rates of tuberculosis incidence and mortality rose alarmingly. After 1941 TB mortality rates in England and Wales fell, but in Scotland they remained high. It was estimated that the death rate from respiratory TB in Scotland at the war's end was almost 50 per cent higher than it would have been had the prewar tendency continued.[23]

The prewar trend towards declining rates of venereal disease was also reversed during the war. The figures for the entire civilian population do not accurately reflect the disease's wartime increase because military service removed large numbers of young men from the civilian ranks. The trend for women may be a more accurate indicator of the wartime pattern: the number of cases in England and Wales seen for the first time rose each year after 1940 and by 1945 were almost double the 1940 total.

By 1942 military leaders had become quite disturbed about the number of soldiers stationed in Britain who were incapacitated by venereal diseases. Under pressure to protect the health of Canadian and US soldiers, the government introduced Regulation 33B, which allowed the authorities to compel a person to undergo examination and treatment when named by two other persons as the source of their infection. Since the regulation applied to men as well as women, the government claimed it had avoided the sex discrimination involved in a similar First World War policy (1.6), but in practice it was almost entirely used against women: of the 417 persons forced to undergo treatment in 1944, 414 were females. The National Council of Women and other groups protested against the government's policy because it seemed to suggest that women were responsible for spreading the disease (1.8, 1.9). Regulation 33B thus contributed to wartime gender conflict.

---

[22] Linda Bryder, *Below the Magic Mountain*, Oxford, 1988, p. 246.
[23] Titmuss, *Problems of Social Policy*, p. 526.

III

The wartime shift towards policies promoting greater equality was especially beneficial to the working class. Price controls and rationing reduced class differences in consumption. Full employment, rent control and food subsidies contributed to a substantial rise in real wages. Compared with the 1930s, the wartime working-class standard of living improved considerably. But the government's claim to have established 'equality of sacrifice' and 'fair shares for all' exaggerates the extent of change; class continued to affect access to food and clothing.[24] The Ministry of Food admitted privately that the food rationing scheme was 'essentially inequitable', in that it provided the same quantity to each person regardless of need; middle-class brain workers benefited since they were allowed the same food ration as working-class employees doing heavy physical labour.[25]

While some experienced a new sense of social unity during the months following Dunkirk, when fear of invasion was strongest, class feeling did not disappear during the war. Home Intelligence reports on public opinion indicate that resentment of the wealthy by lower-income groups was a 'continual theme until the end of the war'.[26] Evacuation often led to class tension as middle-class hosts and working-class evacuees struggled to co-exist under one roof (2.1), while the government's scheme to evacuate children overseas increased class feeling precisely at the time the Dunkirk spirit was said to have created a new sense of solidarity (2.2). Although wartime food rationing did reduce inequality, the public was aware that more and better food continued to be available to those wealthy enough to dine in restaurants (2.11, 2.13) or buy on the black market. A recent study concluded that evacuation increased class feeling among the working-class evacuees, and that this heightened class identification may have increased

---

[24] The official history of civil industry concluded that there was a 'wide disparity' in the way clothes rationing affected different classes. Among the social elite, women increased their wardrobes by 4 per cent between 1942 and 1944 and men by 6 per cent, but in the poorest class women's wardrobes declined by 7 per cent while men's were reduced by 8 per cent. E. L. Hargreaves and M. M. Gowing, *Civil Industry and Trade*, London, 1952, p. 329.

[25] R. J. Hammond, *Food. Vol. I, The Growth of Policy*, London, 1951, p. 125.

[26] Yass, *This Is Your War*, p. 58.

Labour voting in 1945.[27] Some MPs anticipated Labour would do well in the 1945 general election because class resentment had increased (2.15).

Wartime industrial relations also suggest that prewar class conflict continued during the war. Class feeling was so strong in some war factories that management and workers appeared to view each other as a greater enemy than the Germans (2.6). Although illegal after July 1940, unofficial strikes continued to occur in the months following Dunkirk and during the Battle of Britain; close to a million working days were lost to strikes in 1940. The number of industrial disputes and the number of working days lost through strikes increased each year from 1940 through 1944. By 1941 the loss of output due to employer–employee antagonism had become an issue at the highest level of government. Pro-employer ministers warned Churchill that war production was being held back by workers' slackness (2.8). Ernest Bevin, the Minister of Labour, considered these claims a form of class warfare by employers and informed Churchill that they were unfounded rumours (2.9).

IV

If the war created a new sense of social solidarity, it did not include Jews, blacks, the Irish, German and Austrian refugees or Italians living in Britain. At the beginning of the war aliens believed to be Nazi supporters were arrested and interned, but other aliens were left alone. In June 1940, immediately following Dunkirk, there were anti-Italian riots in several British cities[28] and an outburst of public anti-alien feeling which strengthened the position of those within the government who urged mass arrests of aliens without requiring evidence of wrongdoing. In the following months about 27,000 aliens, mainly Central European

[27] Travis Crosby, *The Impact of Civilian Evacuation in the Second World War*, London, 1986, p. 149.
[28] Many of the Italians whose property was attacked by mobs had lived in Britain for years and had no sympathy for Mussolini. Terri Colpi, 'The impact of the Second World War on the British Italian community', in David Cesarani and Tony Kushner (eds), *The Internment of Aliens in Twentieth Century Britain*, London, 1993, pp. 167–87.

refugees who had fled to Britain to escape Nazi persecution, were interned. Many of those arrested were Jews and anti-Semitism may have contributed to the public support for mass arrests. A Mass-Observation survey found 55 per cent of those questioned approved of interning all aliens; 27 per cent thought this should be limited to those who had revealed Nazi sympathies.[29]

Britain had a long tradition of anti-Semitism before 1939 and the stress of war intensified it. Wartime opinion polls consistently revealed public antipathy toward British Jews. Anti-Semitism increased even after the extermination camps in Poland had become public knowledge (3.8). Anti-Semites often attempted to turn public opinion against Jews by claiming they were disproportionately involved in the black market. Although a 1943 government investigation revealed this was untrue, popular anti-Jewish feeling was so deeply entrenched the government refused to publish the survey for fear that it would be seen as pro-Jewish.[30]

The Irish were the largest ethnic group in wartime Britain. Prewar prejudice against them does not appear to have been dissolved by any wartime sense of social solidarity. Because of the labour shortage, the government was anxious that the prewar pattern of migration from southern Ireland into Britain continue despite security concerns. But the use of Irish labour was hampered by hostile stereotypes among government officials and the public (3.1). Housing for Irish workers was a sticky issue. The government's Regional Welfare Officer in Manchester reported: 'The majority of householders in England are strongly unwilling to have Irishmen in their houses as lodgers and it may be very difficult to persuade Local Authorities to compel their citizens to accept Irishmen, even of the better type'.[31] A recent study of the Irish in England concluded that anti-Irish bias provided the 'most striking continuity' linking their prewar and postwar experiences of life in England.[32]

[29] Bernard Wasserstein, *Britain and the Jews of Europe 1939–1945*, Oxford, 1979, p. 94.
[30] Kushner, *The Persistence of Prejudice*, p. 139.
[31] Public Record Office, LAB 26/9, 29 August 1941. Cited in Kenneth Lunn, '"Good for a few hundreds at least": Irish labour recruitment into Britain during the Second World War', in Patrick Buckland and John Belchem (eds), *The Irish in British Labour History*, Liverpool, 1992, p. 109.
[32] Steven Fielding, *Class and Ethnicity: Irish Catholics in England, 1880–1939*, Buckingham, 1993, p. 131.

The concept of social solidarity had little relevance to non-Caucasians in wartime Britain. Racial discrimination existed before the arrival of US soldiers (3.2),[33] but increased during the war as the US Army pressed British authorities to co-operate with its policy of racial segregation. In 1942 the Secretary of State for War, P. J. Grigg, urged the Cabinet to approve his policy of educating British troops to adopt the attitude of the US Army toward black soldiers (3.3). But, while agreeing that Britons should avoid becoming too friendly with black GIs (3.4), the Cabinet objected to the explicit prejudice in Grigg's proposal. It approved a policy that British troops should 'respect' the white US soldiers' point of view, that white and 'coloured' American troops should not be invited to social gatherings at the same time, and that white British women should avoid black soldiers (3.5). Although the British authorities thus avoided an overt commitment to enforce racial segregation, unofficially they did co-operate with the US Army's policy of segregating public facilities. The new racial policies – for example regarding access to pubs, restaurants and cinemas – were also imposed on non-Caucasian Britons, who often resisted; numerous incidences of racial violence resulted.[34]

V

Gender conflict also increased during the war. By 1941 the government had reluctantly decided to mobilise women; the December 1941 National Service (No. 2) Act allowed the government to conscript women into the women's services, munitions factories or civil defence. But while requiring women to assume increasingly masculine roles, the government sought to maintain gender boundaries. Women's groups urged the appointment of women to positions of authority (4.1), but these were generally reserved for

---

[33] Laura Tabili, *'We Ask for British Justice': Workers and Racial Difference in Late Imperial Britain*, Ithaca, 1994.

[34] David Reynolds, 'The Churchill government and the black American troops in Britain during World War II', *Transactions of the Royal Historical Society*, 35, 1985, pp. 122–3. Women in the Auxiliary Territorial Service were ordered not to speak with black GIs unless another white person was present; in some regions local police went so far as to arrest white women for keeping company with black soldiers on the charge that they were doing damage to growing crops.

men. Most women in munitions factories were paid at lower rates than men, and regarded as temporary workers whose employment would be terminated when the war ended. Gender distinctions were also maintained in the women's services. Women were usually assigned jobs, such as cooking or clerical work, consistent with women's traditional roles, and were restricted to non-combatant functions. Women were allowed to operate anti-aircraft batteries, for example, but they were not permitted to fire the guns.[35]

Although women's participation in the war effort was essential to national survival, the government attempted to maintain prewar sex-differentiated policies. Women civil defence workers received two-thirds the man's rate of pay, while the 1939 Personal Injuries (Emergency Provisions) Act granted women injured by enemy action two-thirds the compensation men received. Feminists were quick to point out the contradiction in government policy: women were being required to accept near equality of sacrifice, while still being denied equality of rights. With the support of the Woman Power Committee,[36] the Equal Compensation Campaign Committee conducted a successful campaign to obtain equal compensation for war injuries (4.4, 4.5). The Equal Pay Campaign Committee and the Women's Publicity Planning Association directed unsuccessful campaigns for equal pay (11.8) and for sex equality under the law (4.9).

Women experienced greater sexual freedom during the war, stimulating public alarm that traditional restraints on female sexual activity were dissolving (4.10, 4.11). Women in uniform were often assumed by men to be sexually available (4.13). When rumours of promiscuous sexual behaviour by service women became so widespread that they hampered recruiting for the women's services, the government was forced to appoint a committee to investigate (4.2). Attitudes towards women's increased sexual freedom were gendered. A 1944 Mass-Observation report concluded that the double standard of sexual morality was being undermined. It found that most men regretted the liberalisation of

---

[35] Dorothy Sheridan, 'Ambivalent memories: women and the 1939–45 war in Britain', *Oral History*, 18, 1, 1990, p. 38.
[36] The Woman Power Committee was established in 1940 by the British Federation of Business and Professional Women and back-bench women MPs to protect women's interests. See Harold L. Smith, 'The womanpower problem in Britain during the Second World War', *Historical Journal*, 27, 4, 1984, p. 929.

sexual morality, but that the majority of women welcomed it.[37] Responding to the public's moral concern about female sexual behaviour, and to the perception that this was causing the rise in venereal disease, the government increased efforts to control female sexuality, including sending females up to the age of 23 to borstal for sexual immorality.[38]

During the 1930s the marriage rate had begun to rise, and it accelerated during the war. British women married at a much higher rate and at an earlier age than before the war; these trends continued after 1945. The decline in singleness was especially evident for women aged 25–29: whereas 42 per cent were unmarried in 1931, only 22 per cent in this group were single in 1951. Full employment and changed social policies created favourable conditions for a higher marriage rate, but women's attitudes toward marriage also changed. The generation of young women reaching adulthood during the war viewed marriage much more favourably than their mothers' generation.[39]

Marital conflict may have increased during the war. With their husbands away in the armed forces, wives discovered they could manage on their own; as a result, some looked forward to a greater equality within marriage (5.8). But equality did not extend to eliminating the double standard of sexual relations. Many lonely wives drifted into sexual relationships during the war. While national statistics are not available, married women were responsible for one-third of the illegitimate conceptions in Birmingham during the war's last two years.[40] Although it was accepted that husbands in the armed forces would engage in sexual activity, marital conflict often resulted when wives did so while their husbands were away. Judges upheld the right of husbands to punish their wives physically, even to the point of

---

[37] Sue Harper, 'The representation of women in British feature films, 1939–45', in Philip M. Taylor (ed.), *Britain and the Cinema in the Second World War*, New York, 1988, p. 177.

[38] Harper, 'The representation of women', p. 179.

[39] Jay Winter, 'War, family and fertility in twentieth-century Europe', in John Gillis, *et al.* (eds), *The European Experience of Declining Fertility: A Quiet Revolution 1850–1970*, Oxford, 1992, p. 305. This trend was not due to participation in the war; neutral nations, including Sweden and Switzerland, experienced a similar change.

[40] Ferguson and Fitzgerald, *Studies in the Social Services*, p. 98. While still legally married, some of the women in this group were separated from their husbands.

death (5.9).[41] The number of divorces between 1941 and 1945 was nearly double that between 1936 and 1940, and the unusually high rate continued in the immediate postwar years.[42] Whereas wives initiated the majority of divorces in the interwar period (53 per cent in 1936–40), husbands initiated the majority of divorces during the war (56 per cent 1941–45) and this trend continued after 1945.[43]

With their husbands away in the armed forces, wives assumed greater authority within the family. But this tendency was undermined by the 1943 High Court ruling in the Blackwell case that a married woman's savings were her husband's property, reaffirming that, legally, a wife remained subordinate to her husband (5.6). This endorsement of a husband's authority aroused strong feeling among wives (5.7). Efforts by women's groups to change the law were unsuccessful in part owing to divergent approaches: the Married Women's Association pressed for amendment of the 1882 Married Women's Property Act, whereas the Women's Co-operative Guild urged legislation 'which would secure to every married woman the right to an equal share with her husband in the home, its income and any savings which may accrue from home administration'.[44]

VI

It is difficult to fit the wartime family into the social solidarity model. Wartime concern with family disintegration and the need

[41] Judges were inconsistent in sentencing husbands who killed their wives for having extramarital relations while the husband was away in the armed forces. In a sample reviewed by Edward Smithies, some set the husband free without serving time in prison, while others imposed prison sentences of up to five years. Edward Smithies, *Crime in Wartime: A Social History of Crime in World War II*, London, 1982, p. 163.

[42] Part of the increase in the wartime divorce rate was due to the 1937 change in divorce law, which made it easier to obtain a divorce. The war accelerated the rise in the divorce rate rather causing it: during the two years before the war the annual average rate of divorce was 60 per cent higher than in the last two years before the change in divorce law. Roderick Phillips, *Putting Asunder: A History of Divorce in Western Society*, Cambridge, 1988, p. 529.

[43] A. H. Halsey (ed.), *British Social Trends since 1900*, London, 1988, p. 80. Part of the reason why more divorces were filed by husbands than wives during the war stemmed from the Army's welfare scheme, which made divorce easier and cheaper if initiated by the husband.

[44] Jean Gaffin and David Thoms, *Caring and Sharing: The Centenary History of the Co-operative Women's Guild*, Manchester, 1983, p. 133.

to rebuild the family continued to be expressed in postwar writing about the family. Convictions for child neglect more than doubled during the war; by 1945 the problem was considered so serious that a wide range of proposals for punishing errant parents was being put forward, including flogging and classes in parent craft (5.12). The separation of children from parents by evacuation, the long-term separation of spouses, with husbands away in the armed forces, and the destruction of homes by enemy bombs were all thought to have contributed to the rising divorce and juvenile delinquency rates. The expanding marriage guidance movement at the end of the war reflected increased concern with the fragility of marriage.[45]

The war also substantially increased the number of one-parent families, and reduced the stigma attached to women who chose motherhood without marriage. Before the war 70 per cent of premarital conceptions were legitimised by marriage before the child's birth. But the wartime removal of men into the armed forces reduced the opportunity to do this. Partly for this reason, the illegitimate birth rate for 1940–45 was almost double that for the preceding six years. The rise in illegitimate births was not primarily due to teenage sexual activity; the age groups with the greatest increase in wartime extramaritally conceived maternities were women aged 30–35 (up 41 per cent) and 25–30 (up 24 per cent).[46] Mass-Observation reports suggest that attitudes toward single parenthood changed during the war; more women chose to be single parents and the prewar stigma attached to that status eroded.[47] But the Beveridge Report and the white paper, *Social Insurance*, left unmarried mothers dependent on public assistance unless they had an employment record; by the 1970s they had become one of the larger groups relying on public assistance.

VII

The rise in wartime crime and juvenile delinquency rates also seems inconsistent with the notion of increased social solidarity.

[45] Jane Lewis, 'Public institution and private relationship: marriage and marriage guidance, 1920–1968', *Twentieth Century British History*, 1, 3, 1990, p. 244.
[46] Ferguson and Fitzgerald, *Studies in the Social Services*, pp. 92–4.
[47] Mass-Observation, *Sex, Morality and the Birth Rate*, file report no. 2205, February 1945, Mass-Observation archive, University of Sussex.

During the five years before the war indictable offences known to the police in England and Wales increased by 21 per cent, but between 1939 and 1945 they rose by 57 per cent.[48] Within a few months after Dunkirk the number of looting cases per month brought before London courts had risen from 539 to 1,662. Scotland Yard was sufficiently concerned to form a special anti-looting squad (6.4), and the government extended from three to six months the maximum prison sentence which courts of summary jurisdiction were allowed to impose. The increase in crime was not due to increased activity by professional criminals but to normally law-abiding citizens violating the law. A sample of convicted London looters during the year following Dunkirk revealed that 42 per cent were persons in official positions, such as air raid wardens, auxiliary firemen and policemen (6.4). During the war, crime ceased to be almost exclusively associated with the working class; for the first time white-collar crime became a serious problem.[49] Although it is impossible to determine the size of the wartime black market, contemporaries believed it to be highly organised, with a large-scale distribution system (6.5).

Juvenile delinquency also increased during the war. The number of juveniles found guilty of indictable offences in England and Wales in 1941 was 42 per cent higher than in 1939.[50] After peaking in 1941, the rate declined before rising to a second peak in 1945. The vast majority of cases involved males, but the number of females aged 14–16 charged with indictable offences in 1941 and 1942 was more than double that in 1939.

As public alarm grew, the authorities sought more effective methods of controlling juveniles. Although a 1938 Home Office committee had recommended the abolition of corporal punishment as a court penalty, this form of punishment was revived during the wartime panic over juvenile delinquency. Magistrates responded to the rise in juvenile delinquency by increasing the number of birchings from 58 in 1939 to 546 in 1941 (6.10). The public outcry against the use of corporal punishment following

[48] Smithies, *Crime in Wartime*, p. 2.
[49] Smithies, *Crime in Wartime*, p. 105.
[50] DMG , 'Juvenile delinquency', internal Home Office memorandum (initialled only), CAB 102/790, August 1945, Public Record Office, London.

the birching of two boys in Hereford without allowing them the opportunity to appeal contributed to the sharp decline in birchings during the rest of the war (6.6, 6.10). Public opinion was divided on this; some feared the authorities were abandoning the only effective deterrent to the emergence of juvenile street gangs and 'wanton' damage to property (6.9).

VIII

Planning became a vogue word in the 1930s, and at first the war strengthened its appeal.[51] Pressure for greater planning controls during the 1930s resulted in the appointment of the Royal Commission on the Geographical Distribution of the Industrial Population (Barlow Commission), which reported in 1940. Its recommendation that a central planning authority be established to control urban sprawl and to encourage better regional distribution of industry was welcomed during the early years of the war, when the Blitz made the rebuilding of British cities necessary. It was followed by the Scott and Uthwatt Committee reports, which provided detailed schemes for national planning.

There appeared to be a consensus on the desirability of planning. In February 1941 the government accepted the principle of national planning and a central planning authority; in 1943 the Town and Country Planning Act established a new ministry responsible for national planning; in 1944 a white paper was issued, *The Control of Land Use*, and a second Town and Country Planning Act gave local councils additional planning powers.

But the wartime planning movement is now viewed as an example of how reform was thwarted by powerful interest groups. Landowners were alarmed by the planning discussions, which necessarily proposed limiting their control over their property. After Conservative backbenchers demanded that Lord Reith, the government's leading advocate of planning, be dismissed, he was removed from office. His successors, Lord

---

[51] John Stevenson, 'Planner's moon? The Second World War and the planning movement', in H. L. Smith (ed.), *War and Social Change: British Society in the Second World War*, Manchester, 1986, p. 75.

Portal and later W. S. Morrison, were Conservatives who were aware of the resistance to planning from within their party and who successfully sought to weaken reform proposals. Conservative ministers refused to accept the Uthwatt Committee's key proposal that the state should control development rights. Since Labour considered this essential to planning, it became an important source of party conflict. Party differences ensured that the white paper *The Control of Land Use* was stillborn; disliked by both major parties, it was issued for discussion and then shelved. The 1944 Town and Country Planning Act was only a shadow of what was originally contemplated; instead of granting broad powers necessary for effective planning, it provided local councils authority to rebuild bombed areas within cities. Even so, party conflict over the bill nearly led to the break-up of the coalition government. By 1945 the earlier hopes for bold, comprehensive planning had evaporated as government support for national planning gave way to a concern for 'economizing and protecting private interests'.[52]

IX

In *Social Insurance and Allied Services*, William Beveridge presented a scheme which he claimed would abolish 'want' by providing security against all the main causes of poverty. In addition to being comprehensive in coverage, it was universal – including everyone instead of just the working class – and it provided benefits without a means test. It also claimed that a 'satisfactory' system of social security assumed the introduction of children's allowances, a national health service, and the avoidance of mass unemployment.

Contrary to suggestions that Beveridge proposed a Santa Claus welfare state, in some respects his report was a very conservative document. Treasury opponents of the non-contributory method of financing used in the 1908 Old Age Pensions Act welcomed Beveridge's recommendation that his plan be financed by contributions from workers, employers and the state, rather than

---

[52] Junichi Hasegawa, *Replanning the Blitzed City Centre: A Comparative Study of Bristol, Coventry and Southampton 1941–1950*, Buckingham, 1992, p. 16.

from general taxation. This meant, as Beveridge noted, that instead of redistributing wealth from one class to another, the scheme's main effect would be to transfer resources within the working class from those who were healthy, employed and childless to those who were ill, unemployed and had children (9.3, para. 449). Beveridge proposed flat-rate rather than earnings-related benefits because he was concerned not to undermine individual responsibility. The former would provide a bare subsistence income; Beveridge thought it should be the individual's responsibility to provide for anything above that (9.3, para. 9). Although he proposed that unemployment benefit be of unlimited duration, Beveridge also recommended 'penal treatment' as a last resort for those who failed to comply with the conditions for benefit or assistance (9.3, para. 373).

War may have been good for children and expectant mothers, but it had undesirable consequences for the elderly. The war encouraged the belief that the elderly were a burden on society, that adequate pensions for them would be at the expense of programmes for the young, and that in allocating resources the latter should be given priority. Beveridge shared these assumptions and warned against being too generous to the elderly. The pension rates he recommended were so low (25s per week for a couple, increasing to 40s weekly in 1965) that they did not provide a subsistence income, and Beveridge admitted they would have to be topped up by means-tested supplements. Although the white paper on social insurance proposed introducing the full pension immediately, it lowered the rate even further, to 35s weekly for a couple. Since Beveridge made retirement mandatory in order to receive a pension, this violation of his subsistence principle was surprising, but the result was predictable: by 1954, 27 per cent of pensioner households were receiving means-tested National Assistance supplements.[53]

Although it supported an expansion of the prewar insurance system, the Conservative Party did not welcome Beveridge's scheme. The secret Conservative Party committee Churchill appointed in December 1942 to review the Beveridge Report objected to several key features. It urged that Beveridge's social

[53] John Macnicol, 'Beveridge and old age', in John Hills *et al.* (eds), *Beveridge and Social Security*, Oxford, 1994, pp. 85, 93.

security plan be replaced with a 'social insurance' scheme in which: (1) unemployment benefit as a matter of right should not be paid for more than six months; (2) the level of benefit should be substantially lower than the wage of the lowest-paid worker in order to preserve the incentive to work; and (3) that consideration be given to abandoning Beveridge's principle of universality by concentrating benefits on those in need (9.6).

The 1944 white paper *Social Insurance* accepted most of Beveridge's proposals, but because of Conservative objections his vision of a social security scheme with unlimited duration of benefit payments was abandoned; the white paper's title was chosen to indicate this shift. This signalled the government's rejection of one of Beveridge's basic principles: the abolition of 'want' through adequacy of benefit in amount and in time. In place of Beveridge's principle of a guaranteed subsistence income for an unlimited period, the white paper substituted a 'reasonable insurance against want' (9.12, para. 13). This resulted from the government's refusal to tie rates of benefit to the level needed for a subsistence income. Whereas Beveridge's principle of adequacy was intended to ensure that few people would be dependent on means-tested assistance, the white paper assumed that means testing would have an important role in the new scheme.[54]

The Beveridge Report has been portrayed as an expression of the wartime sense of social solidarity because it extended coverage to all citizens rather than just low-income groups. But under the Beveridge scheme the right to benefits was derived from paid employment, not citizenship. This had important consequences for women: upon marriage they lost their separate identity and derived their eligibility for benefits from their husband's contributions even if they had a previous employment record (9.9). Women without husbands – whether widowed, divorced, separated, or single parents – became one of the most important groups relying upon public assistance in the postwar world, a development which stemmed from Beveridge's decision to base entitlement on paid work rather than on citizenship. Although supporting other parts of the Beveridge Report, Mavis Tate, MP, claimed that 'a more deplorable, reactionary measure in regard to

[54] Alan Deacon and Jonathan Bradshaw, *Reserved for the Poor: The Means Test in British Social Policy*, Oxford, 1983, p. 46.

married women had never been brought forward'.[55] Since wartime and postwar feminist groups protested against this aspect of the Beveridge scheme, it increased gender conflict (9.10).

X

The 1945 Family Allowances Act has been linked to the increased awareness of child poverty arising from evacuation. But the government resisted family allowances as long as it was politically possible, and eventually proceeded for reasons which had little to do with social justice. The war strengthened the pro-natalist case that allowances were needed to stimulate population growth (1.1). When wartime price increases provoked demands for general wage raises, reform advocates presented family allowances as a cheaper alternative to wage increases (10.2). Beveridge's endorsement was decisive in convincing a reluctant government to proceed with reform, but he viewed the allowances as of vital importance because they would ensure that the gap between the earnings of the lowest-paid employed worker and the benefits received by the unemployed would be as large as possible (10.5).

After the principle of family allowances had been accepted, the issue of whether they should be paid to the father or the mother generated gender tension for over a year. Since the First World War, Eleanor Rathbone had been urging for family allowances to be paid to the mother in order to recognise the value of the mother's work, but the government originally intended to have the allowances paid to the father (10.6). This was defended on the ground that it would be undesirable to take any step which might weaken the father's sense of responsibility for maintaining his family. There was also concern that paying the allowance to the mother might imply she was responsible for supporting the child and lead to pressure for increasing the allowance to provide full maintenance. Enraged by what appeared to be a denial of the value of the work performed by mothers, women's groups successfully conducted a campaign to pressure Parliament into agreeing on payment to the mother.[56] After Rathbone warned that

---

[55] *Women in Council Newsletter*, November 1943, p. 3.
[56] Susan Pedersen, *Family, Dependence, and the Origins of the Welfare State: Britain and France, 1914–1945*, Cambridge, 1993, p. 349.

the next general election would be marked by a revival of sex antagonism unless the government changed its policy (10.7), and the House of Commons threatened to revolt, the government gave way and allowed a free vote on the issue.

The 1944 white paper on a national health service has also been cited as evidence of a wartime policy consensus. There was all-party agreement on the need for a comprehensive national health system which would be free at the point of service. But since they have had access to Public Record Office files relating to policy development, historians have focused on the conflicts between the coalition parties over the form the new health service should take. Because these differences were profound and never fully bridged, the white paper was put forward only as a consultative document, not as an agreed basis for legislation.

After the white paper was published, the British Medical Association's lobbying resulted in significant changes in the government's proposals. This transformation after 1944 has been characterised by the official historian of the National Health Service as a process of 'capitulation rather than the emergence of consensus'.[57] It was a highly visible example of reconstruction policy being shaped by a self-interested pressure group rather than by idealistic policy makers influenced by a new wartime social conscience.

When the coalition ended in May 1945, the Conservative caretaker government proceeded to draft a revised national health service scheme (10.15). This 'shattered the fragile consensus' represented by the white paper.[58] The Labour Party subsequently felt free to draft its own scheme. The health service established by the postwar Labour government thus reflected Labour's policy; it was not simply the 1944 white paper implemented.

XI

The 1944 Education Act is often cited as the most important reform legislation actually introduced during the war. It raised the

[57] Charles Webster, *The Health Services Since the War. Vol. I. Problems of Health Care: The National Health Service Before 1957*, London, 1988, p. 392.
[58] Webster, *The Health Services*, p. 80.

school-leaving age to fifteen and mandated free secondary education (except for direct-grant schools) for all in grammar, secondary modern and technical schools, to which children would be assigned by examination at age eleven plus. But recently historians have become more conscious of how much of the prewar system the Act retained. The 1938 Spens Report recommended free secondary education, a tripartite system of secondary education, and the raising of the school-leaving age from fourteen to fifteen.[59] The outbreak of war prevented the latter from going into effect on 1 September 1939 as scheduled.

It was not accidental that the Act restricted educational change. R. A. Butler, the President of the Board of Education, claimed that he was primarily 'codifying existing practice' and providing a legislative basis for proposals that were already widely accepted among educational reformers before the war. He also ensured that the reform would reflect the Conservative Party's views on education: the public schools were protected, direct-grant secondary schools were allowed to continue charging fees, religion was made mandatory in secondary schools, and diversity and variety were to be essential features of state-provided secondary education (11.3, 11.7).

Recent writing on the 1944 Act has portrayed it as a missed opportunity. It perpetuated an educational system which reinforced class divisions: middle-class children continued to attend grammar schools while the majority of working-class children were placed in the secondary modern schools. While ensuring that religion would be a part of secondary education, the Act placed little importance on science and technical education. The Percy Committee issued a report recommending improved provision of higher technological education at the end of the war (11.10), but very little was done in this area in the decade after 1945. Although its relative importance is a matter of dispute, Britain's poor postwar economic performance has been linked to inadequate provision of higher technological education.[60]

---

[59] *Report of the Consultative Committee on Secondary Education with Special Reference to Grammar Schools and Technical High Schools*, London, 1938.
[60] Correlli Barnett, *The Audit of War: The Illusion and Reality of Britain as a Great Nation*, London, 1986.

XII

The 1944 white paper *Employment Policy* has been portrayed as a turning-point in economic policy in that the government appeared to have committed itself to maintaining full employment by using Keynesian methods. The white paper is thus often assumed to have been the basis for postwar government policies which were thought responsible for the high level of employment after 1945.

Recent studies have cast doubt on this approach. Beveridge was preparing a report in 1944 which was expected to recommend a full-employment policy. The white paper was rushed into print to pre-empt Beveridge's more radical proposal. The white paper avoided a commitment to full employment, substituting in its place a modest pledge to maintain a high and stable level of employment (12.4).[61] Rather than accepting Keynesian methods to accomplish this, it adopted contradictory positions on demand management: deficit spending was explicitly rejected in section 74 but accepted in section 77. Postwar employment policy was not based on the white paper's specific proposals, and the 1947 economic crisis is now viewed as the point at which the government adopted Keynesian economics.[62]

The employment white paper has been considered an example of the wartime policy consensus between the coalition parties. This is misleading; the white paper was a compromise which neither Labour nor the Conservatives welcomed. The Parliamentary Labour Party agreed only to the principle that the government should accept responsibility for the maintenance of full employment; it explicitly refused to endorse the specific proposals presented in the white paper (12.5). In its 1945 election manifesto the Conservative Party pledged itself to maintaining a 'high and stable' level of employment rather than the Labour policy of full employment.

---

[61] Although the white paper did not specify what rate of unemployment was consistent with its goal of a 'high' level of employment, the Chancellor of the Exchequer considered 8.5 per cent an appropriate objective and the white paper's appendix mentions 8 per cent.

[62] Alan Booth, *British Economic Policy, 1931–49*, Brighton, 1989, p. 55.

XIII

The traditional view that the war stimulated a consensus on the expansion of state activity pays insufficient attention to the reaction against collectivism which intensified during the war's final years. Several pressure groups emerged dedicated to defending the 'free enterprise' system: Aims of Industry, the Progress Trust, the National League of Freedom, and the Society of Individualists. These groups were supported by prominent Conservatives, including Ralph Assheton, who became Conservative Party Chairman in 1944, A. G. Erskine-Hill, Chairman of the Conservative Party's back-bench 1922 Committee, and Henry Willink, Minister of Health from 1943 to 1945.

Consensus historians have viewed the 1945 general election as a contest between parties in broad agreement on domestic policy and have attributed Labour's victory to its conveying a sense of greater determination to implement those policies. But this ignores the intense ideological conflict dividing Labour and the Conservatives during the war's final year. Churchill's 1945 election address, in which he claimed that socialism and economic controls would lead to political tyranny (12.8), was an expression of this fundamental ideological conflict. His comments were not an aberration, but reflected the Conservative opposition to collectivism which Friedrich A. Hayek articulated in his 1944 book, *The Road to Serfdom* (12.7).

Conservative Party leaders welcomed Hayek's book because it provided them with a theoretical critique of the collectivism they had reluctantly tolerated as the price of maintaining a coalition government.[63] After he became Conservative Party Chairman, Ralph Assheton drew upon Hayek's book in his speeches, sent copies of those speeches to Churchill, and encouraged Churchill to use Hayek's ideas.[64] Whether Churchill read Hayek's book is unclear, but Hayek's ideas were available to him when he drafted his election speech; in addition to Assheton, other prominent

[63] Among those who read Hayek's book was a Somerville College chemistry student who, as Margaret Thatcher, conducted a sustained assault on the principles of the welfare state after she became Prime Minister in 1979.
[64] Richard Cockett, *Thinking the Unthinkable: Think-Tanks and the Economic Counter-Revolution 1931–1983*, London, 1994, p. 92.

Conservatives also forwarded summaries of Hayek's ideas to Churchill.[65] The Conservative Party considered Hayek's message so important they asked his publisher to issue an abridged edition of the book before the election and offered a large quantity of their own paper ration to make this possible.[66] Although the Conservative Party was prepared to expand the prewar social services if it won the election, the behaviour of the 1945 Conservative 'caretaker' government and the statements of Conservative Party leaders during the election suggest it was the 1945 election defeat, rather than the war, which led to the postwar Conservative acceptance of full employment and Labour's version of the welfare state.

Wartime emergency conditions increased public support for an expansion of state-provided social services, but did not necessarily imply that this would continue in peacetime. Some opponents thought it inappropriate to launch full-scale attacks on the reform proposals while the war was still in progress. Ernest Benn, President of the Society of Individualists, noted in his diary that while his group was strongly opposed to the wartime trend toward collectivism, it was reluctant to 'indulge in too much criticism while the war lasts' because it did not want to undermine national unity.[67] Evidence such as this led Jose Harris to conclude that the war created an 'artificial sense' of social solidarity, which 'encouraged the largely false expectation that much of the emergency apparatus of control, direction and demotion of private goals would be permanently acceptable'.[68]

---

[65] See the correspondence in the Public Record Office, PREM 4/88/2.
[66] Cockett, *Thinking the Unthinkable*, p. 93.
[67] Ernest Benn diary entry, 1 July 1941. Cited in Deryck Abel, *Ernest Benn: Counsel for Liberty*, London, 1960, p. 105.
[68] Jose Harris, 'Political ideas and the debate on state welfare, 1940–45', in H. L. Smith (ed.), *War and Social Change: British Society in the Second World War*, Manchester, 1986, p. 256.

1

Demography and health

Prewar concern with the declining rate of population growth increased during the war. This contributed to the growing support for family allowances and was directly responsible for the appointment of the Royal Commission on Population. During the war the government intervened much more actively to maintain public health. Despite some setbacks during the early years, after 1942 the health of the population improved. Tuberculosis (TB) and venereal disease (VD) remained particularly troublesome areas. While the Blitz has been the focus of public attention, the number of civilians killed by TB in 1940 exceeded deaths in that year from enemy action.[1]

1.1 Beveridge on population

The Beveridge Report revived public concern about the perceived population problem and proposed 'children's allowances' as part of the solution.

117. In the next thirty years housewives as Mothers have vital work to do in ensuring the adequate continuance of the British race....

413. In addition ... there are arguments [for children's allowances] arising from consideration of numbers of population and care of children. With its present rate of reproduction, the British race cannot continue; means of reversing the recent course of the birth rate must be found. It is not likely that allowances for children or any other economic incentives will, by themselves,

---

[1] There were 28,144 deaths from tuberculosis in England and Wales in 1940, whereas 23,186 civilians lost their lives as a result of enemy action in that year. Richard Titmuss, *Problems of Social Policy*, London, 1950, p. 559.

provide that means and lead parents who do not desire children to rear children for gain. But children's allowances can help restore the birth rate....

Social Insurance and Allied Services, Cmd 6404, London, 1942, pp. 53, 154.

1.2 Threat of population decline

The declining rate of population growth was viewed with considerable alarm, as it would have consequences for the economy and the armed forces as well as the age structure of the population if it continued.

Without going into the mass of statistics, the central fact is that we are not replacing our stock. The White Paper does not deny this. Unless we can change this trend in the population, two things will happen to the population of the nation. First, it will decline by something like one-quarter every 30 years.... Secondly, we have to consider the consequences which flow from that fact. There will be a great change in the position of the age groups of the population. In 1901 in this country there were more than five children under 15 for every person of pensionable age. There were five children growing up for every adult declining at the end of life. In 1961 there will be only one child at school for every pensioner in the eventide of life, and in 1971 there will be three pensioners for every two children at school....

That change in the age composition of the nation presents an enormous problem, which deserves the full attention of this House [of Commons], of the Government and of the nation. If the Debate serves no other purpose than to focus attention upon this question, it will have been worth while. Why is it that population is declining? I think the central fact is that over an increasing proportion of our population children are no longer a matter of chance but have become a matter of choice. That has been true of the middle and upper classes for more than a generation, and it is now true of the working class.

James Griffiths, *Hansard, Parliamentary Debates*, fifth series, vol. 391, 16 July 1943, cc. 565–6.

1.3   Royal Commission on Population

Under pressure from the House of Commons, the government appointed a Royal Commission on Population to
examine current population trends and to make recommendations. Because of the concern over the declining rate
of population growth, it was assumed that these would be
designed to stimulate a more rapid rate of growth.

In his broadcast on Reconstruction last February [1943], the
Prime Minister said: '... If this country is to keep its high place in
the leadership of the world and to survive as a great power that
can hold its own against external pressure, our people must be
encouraged by every means to have larger families.'

Thus it is no longer an open question whether the threatened
decline in our population is undesirable, or whether it is an object
of Government policy to raise the replacement rate. I shall
assume, therefore, that the main function of the enquiry will be to
elucidate the factual bases, and suggest the lines, of a positive
population policy. Such a policy would have to take account of
influences on the quality of our population, but its main emphasis
would presumably be on ways of checking the threatened decline
in quantity.

'The form of the population inquiry', memorandum by the Paymaster
General (Lord Cherwell), 1943, MH 58/407, Public Record Office,
London.

1.4   Conservative population policy

Wartime pro-natalism was especially evident in the Conservative Party general election manifesto.

Motherhood must be our special care. There must be a large
increase of maternity beds and convalescent homes, and they
must be provided in the right places. Mothers must be relieved of
onerous duties which at such times so easily cause lasting injury
to their health. The National Insurance Scheme will make financial provision for these needs. All proper arrangements, both
voluntary and State-aided, must be made for the care of other

young children in the family, in order that the energies of the male breadwinner or the kindness of neighbours and relations, which nevertheless must be the mainspring, should not be unduly burdened. Nursery schools and nurseries such as have grown up during the war should be encouraged. On the birth, the proper feeding and the healthy upbringing of a substantially increased number of children, depends the life of Britain and her enduring glory.

'Mr. Churchill's declaration of policy to the electors' (Conservative Party 1945 general election manifesto), in F. W. S. Craig (ed.), *British General Election Manifestos 1900–1974*, London, 1975, p. 118.

1.5 Meals for schoolchildren

Education authorities viewed the school meals programme as an important step toward improving children's health. But the children receiving the food did not always view the matter in the same light.

May I draw attention to the ... remarks [in the social security debate] that the provision of school meals will prove beneficial to both parents and children?

As one of these children I venture to protest....

Being one of those who have rebelliously partaken of grey badly-peeled potatoes, an over-abundance of partially cooked parsnips and turnips, and thick cold grisly slabs of meat, I find myself incapable of enthusiasm for this payment in kind. The continued non-appearance of green vegetables was, and is, the cause of much objective speculation....

Puddings alternated between tapioca and suety duff, of which the former could be proved by experiment to be possessed of enormous powers of adhesion by the simple method of turning the plate upside down.

Hordes of disgruntled schoolfellows will agree when I mention the cold lumpy porridge, and the greasy plateful of chipped bacon and solid fried bread for breakfast.... At tea-time ... one often remarks rather forcibly the conspicuous absence of the jam ration. Jam yesterday, jam tomorrow, but never jam today....

This is only a comment from a child's angle, but if this clause on payment in kind is inserted surely it would help if an inspector of school meals could be supplied.

Phyllis Cannell, letter to the editor, *Time and Tide*, 25, 18 November 1944, pp. 1011–12.

1.6 Government policy on venereal disease

The venereal disease rate rose rapidly as the number of foreign troops stationed in Britain increased, and military leaders pressed the British government to take steps to prevent soldiers from being incapacitated. The government responded by taking new powers to compel a person to undergo examination and, if infected, treatment.

2. Our proposal is that compulsory powers should be conferred by Defence Regulation on Medical Officers of Health to require the examination and, if necessary, the treatment of persons who are named as the source of infection by two separate patients under treatment....

15. Canadian Military Headquarters have made representations to the War Office–

'For many months past the Canadian Corps Commander and this Headquarters have watched the increase in Venereal Diseases among Canadian Troops with the greatest anxiety.... Whenever possible we have endeavoured to identify and trace the source of infection, and in many cases it has been determined that one woman has been the cause of a multiplicity of cases....'

20. The Regulation now proposed is on quite a different basis from the Regulation 40D which was made in February 1918, and which aroused considerable opposition. It does not attempt to deal with prostitution or soliciting but only with the treatment of infectious cases and it does not discriminate against women.

'Venereal disease', memorandum by the Minister of Health (Ernest Brown), 14 October 1942, CAB 71/10, Public Record Office, London.

1.7   Regulation 33B fair to women?

Seeking to avoid a repetition of the controversy which had
resulted from Regulation 40D in the First World War, the
Minister of Health portrayed the proposed Regulation 33B
as a public health measure which did not discriminate
against women.

The Minister of Health [Ernest Brown] explained that the
proposed Regulation dealt with this matter solely as a matter of
public health. Every endeavour had been made to deal with it in a
way to avoid raising controversial issues. In particular, he was
indebted to Parliamentary Counsel for having drafted the
Regulation in such a way that it was not open to objection on the
ground that it appeared to involve discrimination between men
and women.

Lord President's Committee minute, 16 October 1942, CAB 71/7, LP (42)
63, Public Record Office, London.

1.8   Feminists and Regulation 33B

Despite the government's claim that Regulation 33B did not
discriminate against women, feminists thought it was
primarily intended to protect men from infected women.
After the regulation was put into effect almost all the
persons forced to undergo treatment by the regulation were
female.

In rising to move this Prayer, I would make it clear that I am
against the proposed Regulation because I am convinced that it
would be quite ineffective and that, by introducing it, the
Minister of Health is toying with an important problem which we
have in our midst and which is a menace to the public health of
the country....
During the last year [1942], 70,000 new cases of venereal
disease have applied to our civilian clinics for treatment. There
must still be thousands who are not obtaining treatment or who
have not been traced.... We must add to that figure members of

the Forces, since the 70,000 include only those who are receiving treatment in civilian clinics....

If hon. Members accept the Regulation, they will not protect the men and the country from venereal disease, but will meekly accept a third-rate measure which will not give protection against those insidious enemies, syphilis and gonorrhoea, which are more devastating to the health and happiness of the country than Hitler's bombs. Therefore I ask hon. Members to face the question, to realise that the casualties during the last year from venereal disease were far greater than the casualties of the blitz, and to say, 'Let us have only measures which can be regarded as effective and efficient.'...

What is this miserable little measure that has been introduced? Regulation 33B will provide for the treatment of individuals who have infected two others. Nothing more.... No two men will inform upon a respectable woman who has been infected innocently. This regulation will get only a few people, probably only prostitutes, and a few other unfortunate women. The vast number of victims who are infected are left – ignored....

My final point concerns the women who are informed against. Probably most of them will be prostitutes. I want the House to think of the unfortunate, and probably stupid, girl who has become infected, who is informed against by a second man, who is anxious to protect the woman who has in fact infected him. It may be that a girl will be wrongly informed against. The result will be that she is labelled as an immoral woman.... If this Regulation is introduced, it will not only be ineffective, but it may cause hardship and injustice to some unfortunate woman.

Edith Summerskill, *Hansard, Parliamentary Debates*, fifth series, vol. 385, 15 December 1942, cc. 1807–8, 1813.

1.9 Women protest against the venereal disease policy

Women's groups, such as the National Council of Women (NCW), protested against Regulation 33B because it encouraged the perception that it was women who were responsible for the increase in venereal disease. The NCW passed the following resolution at its October 1943 annual conference.

The National Council of Women repudiates as fallacious the prevalent opinion that it is the conduct of girls and women which is mainly responsible for the present increase of Venereal Disease, and desires to emphasise the fact that in the great majority of those fleeting and irresponsible sex relationships by which the disease is spread both partners must be held responsible, and a recall to moral responsibility must necessarily be made to both sexes.

The N.C.W. therefore calls upon the Government to consider afresh its whole approach to this problem, and to initiate a bold and positive educational campaign which will bring home to every citizen and every household the conviction that all who indulge in sexual promiscuity not only may be responsible for the spread of Venereal Disease, but are lacking in good citizenship.

Mrs. Forster (for the Association for Moral and Social Hygiene) said that the [above] resolution was concerned with the problem of irregular sex relationships. Public opinion and the Press laid the blame on the woman. Giving an instance in a district where there were large concentrations of troops one report said that forty girls under sixteen were waiting to go into a Home, and it added 'little blame should be apportioned to the troops'. Girls were the menace and men the victims!... Yet how grossly immoral men could be towards girls, many of them young children, was abundantly proved in charges which came before the Courts.

Women in Council Newsletter, November 1943, p. 6.

1.10 Public reaction to the venereal disease campaign

Alarmed at the rapidly rising venereal disease rate, in October 1942 the government launched a publicity campaign describing the symptoms and transmission of venereal disease. This was considered a bold step, as public references to 'sexual intercourse' were taboo and the government was uncertain as to how the public would react.

An analysis of men's and women's attitudes shows no statistically significant differences between the sexes.

Summary of Results

However, it may be said first that 86% of those interviewed had seen the V.D. statement and 72% said they had read it through.

Taken as a whole the results show that about two-thirds of those interviewed were informed about V.D. to the extent of knowing what the diseases were and how they were spread.

69% said that they knew what the venereal diseases were when asked, and 70% knew, or most probably knew, that the diseases were spread through sexual intercourse.

Not all the informants were asked what the symptoms were, but of the 67% of the sample asked this question, half named the symptoms, or at least one symptom, and a further 17% thought they knew what the symptoms were without describing them....

The vast majority of those interviewed (92%) agreed with the publication of the V.D. statement, and thought it was right for people to be informed about V.D.

'The campaign against venereal disease', Wartime Social Survey, April 1943, RG 23/38, Public Record Office, London.

1.11   Health trends

> Although the government claimed the health of the population improved dramatically during the war, the Minister of Health acknowledged there was a 'considerable increase' in short-term sickness and that the percentage of persons who thought their health had worsened during the war was much higher than those who felt it had improved.

The reports of increasing minor illness which came to notice at various times during the year emanated from many parts of the country. They were of a very general nature and told of crowded surgeries and out-patient departments, more absenteeism due to sickness, and more complaints by individuals of fatigue or feeling 'run down'.

Sickness benefit claims on Approved Societies under the National Health Insurance Scheme were materially above the pre-war average; this is true of all four quarters of the year and is not accounted for by any epidemic. After making due allowance for members of the armed forces, these claims suggest a considerable increase per head in short-term sickness....

It may not be irrelevant to mention that in July and August, 1942, the Wartime Social Survey of the Ministry of Information undertook on behalf of the Ministry [of Health] an enquiry into the public attitude towards health and, in particular (as a measuring rod of interest in health education), to the autumn health publicity which in the last two years has sought to emphasise the dangers of droplet infection. In all 1,795 people were interviewed, and, in accordance with the practice of the Wartime Social Survey, they were carefully chosen to make up a representative sample of the whole population. Some 53 per cent. of those interviewed thought their health was the same as before the war, 10 per cent. thought they were better, and 37 per cent. worse or slightly worse. These answers are obviously highly subjective and must be treated with reserve.

'Summary report of the Ministry of Health for the year ended 31 March, 1943', *Parliamentary Papers 1942–43*, vol. 4, Cmd 6468, London, 1943, pp. 7–8.

1.12   Health of the people

> Although the government believed the wartime diet for most people was an improvement over the prewar period – and for low-income groups this was clearly true – the public tended to attribute ill-health to what they considered to be an inadequate diet.

The 'low state of health' of many people is commented on in three Regions and also Postal Censorship reports. The wartime diet is regarded as the main cause; and to this are ascribed skin troubles, 'flu with bronchial or pneumonic symptoms, and the inability of people to throw off chills.

Venereal disease: The campaign against venereal disease is referred to in five reports this week. Wholehearted approval of the airing of the subject and the demand for more factual information are reported. The Press advertising is generally praised.

'Health', Home Intelligence report, 11 March 1943, INF 1/292, Public Record Office, London.

1.13   Public health better than ever?

During the war the Ministry of Health repeatedly claimed
the health of the British people was better than it had been
before the war. While there is some justification for this
view, opinion surveys indicate the public was sceptical.

Complaints of physical and nervous fatigue have been reported
frequently during the past month. Absenteeism and industrial
unrest are attributed partly to the strain of long working hours
combined with extra Civil Defence and household duties. Many
feel the need of a 'real holiday' – women workers who are
'carrying on a double job' being particularly mentioned.

People are inclined to blame 'vitamin deficiency in the wartime
diet' for the prevalence of skin troubles, indigestion, colds and
general debility, and to feel some resentment of official statements
that 'the health of the nation is better than before the war'.

Tuberculosis: There is comment on the growing fear of an
increase in tuberculosis. The distribution of dirty milk in Derby,
reported earlier in the month, is still a cause for anxiety.

Maternity cases: The shortage of accommodation for maternity
cases is reported (three Regions). 'Expectant mothers have
sometimes to travel at least twenty-five miles for free hospital
accommodation'.

'Health', Home Intelligence report, 24 June 1943, INF 1/292, Public
Record Office, London.

1.14   Maternity care

Wartime maternal and infant mortality rates declined, but
class differences in maternity care remained.

In all aspects of maternity care well-to-do mothers get better
attention than those who are poor. They come under antenatal
supervision earlier, can afford a nursing home bed if no hospital
one is available, and are more often given analgesia. While the
well-to-do owe their privileges largely to being able to afford
private care, they are also more aware of the need for medical
supervision during and after pregnancy, and are seldom prevented

by household ties from making the maximum use of the services available. They have, on the average, fewer children than poor mothers, are more able to obtain domestic help during pregnancy and the lying-in period and retain it for a longer time. There is, however, in all classes room for improvement in the standard of maternity care and domestic help.

Joint Committee of the Royal College of Obstetricians and Gynaecologists and the Population Investigation Committee, *Maternity in Great Britain*, Oxford, 1948, pp. 207–8.

1.15   Tuberculosis allowances

In 1943 the government agreed to grant allowances to persons with tuberculosis so that they would not seek employment and infect others. But in order to minimise the cost, only those considered curable were granted the allowances; those with chronic tuberculosis were ineligible, thus forcing them into the labour force.

It is just over a year since the report of the Medical Research Council's committee on tuberculosis in wartime was published. Its main recommendations – early diagnosis by mass radiography, prompter treatment by an extension of sanatorium accommodation and the completion of a cure by the grant of special allowances to encourage sufferers to be treated and to permit them to stay away from work until they are cured – were accepted by the Government, and it was thought that a campaign against TB was under way. Yet as soon as the scheme for granting allowances was put into force, it became apparent that the Ministry of Health was determined to be as cheeseparing as possible. Since the distinction between the curable case, which is eligible for an allowance, and the chronic case, which is not, was pointed out ... a storm of protest has been made in press and in Parliament – but the Ministry of Health's only reply is that the scheme is only intended to enable persons to give up work temporarily for treatment, and cannot include those whom further treatment will not benefit. When it is pointed out that this places medical officers of health and others who administer the allowances in the invidious position of telling a TB sufferer that he is ineligible for an allowance because he is incurable, the Ministry of Health says that such a person is always eligible for assistance from the local authority – which in most cases means the public assistance that, whether curable cases or not, TB persons will go to any lengths to avoid. In other words, quite apart from the inhumanity involved in telling a person that he is incurable, the Ministry of Health is encouraging chronic cases to find work even if they have positive sputum and are likely to spread the disease among their fellow workers.

'The tuberculosis scandal', *The Economist*, 145, 20 November 1943, pp. 673–4.

1.16   Public health

> Opinion surveys suggested widespread public concern about the wartime spread of tuberculosis and the government's policy toward chronic sufferers.

Government statements about the good health of the nation continue to meet with criticism (Six Regions). In the Southern Region it is pointed out that statistics cannot take into account the number of people who, although not fit, are conscientiously at work, whereas under normal conditions they would be away under doctors' orders.

Tuberculosis (Six Regions): Concern continues at the increase in tuberculosis. It is thought that the exclusion of chronic T.B. sufferers from the Government allowance will cause hardship and that it is 'a blot on a civilised country'.

'Health', Home Intelligence report, 9 December 1943, INF 1/292, Public Record Office, London.

2
Class

Although there is some evidence of reduced class feeling in the months immediately following Dunkirk, this is based largely on the perceptions of middle-class observers and may exaggerate the degree of change. The following selections suggest that class feeling continued to be important throughout the war and may have contributed to the 1945 Labour general election victory.

2.1 Evacuation and class

Although many families welcomed evacuated children into their homes, class differences between the host families and the evacuees affected how they viewed each other.

Mothers of Pre-school Children.

I think this scheme is impracticable and unworkable, and it can never be successful. The low, slum type form the majority of the mothers, some out for what they can get, most of them dirty, many of them idle and unwilling to work or pull their weight. No arrangements whatever have been made for them by the local authorities from the social point of view. They have nowhere to go and walk the streets tiring out themselves and their tiny children....

The general feeling is the people can cope with the children and in time can get them clean and disciplined, but the mothers who are not a good influence are a great drawback....

There is nowhere for them to go. That they are a bad slum type and expect the 'pub and pictures' on the doorstep is not the point. Some arrangements should be made immediately for a Mothers' Club or recreation room for them....

I feel that the dirt and low standard of living of the evacuees from big industrial cities of Leeds and Hull has been an eye-opener and an unpleasant shock to the inhabitants of an agricultural county like Lincolnshire, who had no idea that such terrible conditions existed.

'Preliminary report on evacuation of children and others to Lindsey (Lincs.)', memorandum by Lily Boys, county organiser of Women's Voluntary Services for Civil Defence, 13 September 1939, HLG 7/74, Public Record Office, London.

2.2 Overseas evacuation

When Britain was threatened with invasion in 1940, wealthy people were able to evacuate their children abroad to safety while lower-income groups could not. This increased feelings of class animosity at the time the Dunkirk spirit was said to be uniting Britons.

There is great disappointment at the postponement of the plan for evacuating children to the Dominions. There was initial resistance among the public to sending children abroad: vigorous publicity overcame that resistance, and the results of a statistical survey showed that the parents of approximately 1,000,000 children were prepared for them to go. The effect of a reversal of policy has promoted sharp recrimination against the rich, whose children were enabled to sail.

'Overseas evacuation of children', Home Intelligence report, 16 July 1940, INF 1/264, Public Record Office, London.

2.3 Class and divorce

The demand for divorce increased substantially during the war. Resentment at the class differences in its availability grew accordingly.

There is a considerable increase in the number of people seeking a divorce. This is stated to be due to hasty and ill-considered marriages, thanks to the imminence of calling up, or to one of a couple, who have lived apart for many years, now wishing to marry a member of the Forces. The number of Poor Persons' Lawyers is greatly reduced, and as a result, many people are having to wait over a year before their cases can be begun. Richer people who can afford the minimal cost of £50 can have their cases heard at once, and this naturally leads to much class ill-feeling.

'Divorce', Home Intelligence report, 21–28 May 1941, INF 1/292, Public Record Office, London.

2.4   Evacuation and the 'big houses'

Although some owners of large country houses took in evacuees, many did not and local billeting officers were reluctant to press the issue for fear of repercussions against themselves.

Although there is a fairly general feeling 'that billeting should not be left in the hands of the local agents', (this is very strongly felt in some areas) there is no agreement as to what might be a better arrangement. Some think the power to appoint billeting officers should be transferred from local authorities to the County Councils. Others think that they should be responsible to, and appointed by, a Government Department.

It is frequently suggested that the owners of large country houses are shirking their billeting responsibilities. This is said to be the 'cause of perpetual minor grievances in many districts'. Stories are told of billeting officers who say: 'If this goes on, I shall have to start on some of the big houses'. In another case the officer is alleged to have discouraged the man who was anxious to take evacuees by telling him that, in doing so, he would be 'letting down' owners of other large houses in the neighbourhood.

Complaints, however are by no means confined to large houses. Enquiries in one area suggest that 'there is far more persistent difficulty and resentment regarding the 5–7 bedroom type of house where the occupant is a person of some local consequence whom the billeting officer or local council do not wish to offend'. A reliable report states that, in one area, out of twelve billeting officers, 'only two would face up to the occupant who was unwilling to accept evacuees'.

'Evacuation', Home Intelligence report, 18–25 June 1941, INF 1/292, Public Record Office, London.

2.5   Upper-class women and war work

Upper-class women engaged in voluntary war work were often able to avoid being conscripted into munitions factories or the women's services, and this generated feelings of class resentment.

There is 'considerable resentment among women who are already working that the middle and upper classes are still being allowed to "get away" with voluntary war-jobs as drivers, helpers in canteens, etc.', which can be made to look like whole-time work – 'but if such women want time off, there is never any difficulty with their getting it'. (This is contrasted with the great difficulty experienced by women factory-workers in doing their household shopping. This problem is causing 'more and more discontent' and is thought to be 'seriously holding up the supply of woman-power'. Trades Union representatives again complain that 'very few factories are giving facilities for shopping to their women workers'.) The opinion appears to be general that compulsion is most needed 'among the women-folk of the income groups in which the wage earner is receiving from £400 upwards'.

'Upper-class women and conscription', Home Intelligence report, 27 August – 3 September 1941, INF 1/292, Public Record Office, London.

2.6   Industrial conflict

During 1941 Mass-Observation found prewar class conflict in northern factories continuing unaffected by any Dunkirk spirit.

The most striking feature of the industrial situation here is the survival of strictly peacetime procedure in the conflict between employers and men, which is still today the predominant conflict here. One looked and listened in vain for any sign of a unity binding all parties in the fight against Germany. From the men, one got the fight against the management. From the management, one experienced hours of vituperation against the men. Both sides claim to be concerned only with improving the situation to increase the strength of the struggle against Fascism, but nevertheless, the real war which is being fought here today is still pre-war, private and economic.

Mass-Observation, *People in Production*, London, 1942, p. 15.

2.7 Wartime class conflict

Prewar patterns of conflict between employers and employees continued in Liverpool during the war, despite efforts to promote social unity.

The workers' idea (possibly distorted) of the employers' attitude to the war effort appears important. It seems their patriotism is over-shadowed by their unwillingness to make profits for employers whom they regard as their natural enemies. Propaganda impressing workers of their importance, rather than encouraging their war effort, appears merely to incite them to use their increased bargaining power, whilst the recent publicity given to slacking in factories is regarded as an organised attempt by capitalists to throw the blame on workers to cover their own short-comings. Keen workers with too little to do are said to be suffering from a sense of frustration which is leading to the feeling 'What's the use'?

'Labour problems – Merseyside', appendix to Home Intelligence special report, 3–10 June 1941, INF 1/292, Public Record Office, London.

2.8 Slackness by workers?

If there was a greater sense of social unity in the months immediately following Dunkirk, it had evaporated by 1941 as managers and workers continued to snipe at each other across the class divide.

For some time I have heard from various industrialists with whom I am in touch stories that the workers in various vital industries are no longer putting forward their best efforts, and that there is an increasing slackness becoming apparent. In the last week or two such statements have become more numerous and are now coming to me from men in whose judgment I rely, and I feel therefore obliged to pass on this information.

The remedy suggested is always the same, namely that you should make a personal broadcast to the labour employed in vital industries, urging them to put forward an effort comparable to what they did last year.

Oliver Lyttelton (President of the Board of Trade) to Winston Churchill, 17 June 1941, PREM 4/40/4, Public Record Office, London.

2.9 Worker lethargy

> While admitting that workers were not working as hard as they had in the months following Dunkirk, Bevin, Minister of Labour and National Service, suggested this may have been due to diminished caloric intake rather than un-willingness to work hard as some employers claimed.

It seems to be a case of one person telling another until they have made each other believe it.

That there is a lethargy due to mainly physical conditions is true. We have run the food supply too low for the people on these heavy metal industries; their energy has been sapped and no appeals can make up for it.

Ernest Bevin to Winston Churchill, 23 June 1941, PREM 4/40/4, Public Record Office, London.

2.10 Industrial morale

> Even Bevin admitted that industrial workers showed little awareness of participating in a great national purpose or of the social idealism supposedly generated by the Dunkirk spirit.

All the reports show that there is no defeatism and very little evidence of war weariness. Hard work, alterations in mode of life and various inconveniences are accepted as a necessary part of the war effort....

But in the absence of military operations close to the country there is no fiery enthusiasm or sense of urgency among workers collectively.... The possibility of defeat has not entered the heads of most workers, with the result that they are carrying on quietly rather than urgently, more interested and concerned with their personal interests, their pay packets, their trade union activities, politics after the war, their food and minor comforts. They are anxious for victory but do not see the war as a major issue in their individual lives. There is not sufficient consciousness of their personal responsibility for achieving victory and of the need therefore to sacrifice their personal interests.

'Industrial morale', memorandum by Ernest Bevin, 6 October 1942, CAB 71/10, LP (42) 222, Public Record Office, London.

2.11 'Big bugs' and 'poor beggars'

> The food rationing scheme has been portrayed as the epitome of the idea of fair shares for all, but contemporaries did not necessarily view it that way.

Inequality of Sacrifice

There is growing evidence of a feeling among certain sections of the public that 'everything is not fair and equal and that therefore our sacrifices are not worth while'. In particular, there is some belief that the rich are less hit by rationing than 'ordinary people' for the following reasons:

(a) They can eat at expensive restaurants.
(b) They can afford to buy high priced goods in short demand, such as salmon and game.
(c) They can spend more on clothes and therefore use their coupons more advantageously.
(d) They receive preferential treatment in shops, as 'people giving large orders are favoured and the poorer people wanting "little bits" are refused'.

(e) They receive preferential treatment as regards petrol rationing. To quote a Postal Censorship report: 'we can see the Big Bugs riding in their posh cars and poor beggars can't get petrol for business'.

The feeling of 'inequality of sacrifice' between the Services and civilians, frequently mentioned in these reports, continues. Ill-feeling between the two is said to be growing as tales of slacking in factories, high wages, and black markets increase the belief among Service men that civilians are not pulling their weight.

'Inequality of sacrifice', Home Intelligence report, 25 March 1942, INF 1/292, Public Record Office, London.

2.12 Food and inequality

Because meals in restaurants were outside the rationing scheme, it was possible for those who could afford them to eat more and better food than those limited to rationed items.

I went to see the Chancellor of the Exchequer about luxury feeding in restaurants. There is a great press outcry about meals in expensive hotels, the conclusion being that people who pay 10s. or thereabouts for a meal must be getting a good deal of food for that money, and there's agitation abroad about the inequality of a system that allows wealthy people to feed very adequately off [outside] the ration. We shall have to do something about this, but I don't think the solution is a tax on meals.

Lord Woolton, diary entry, 25 March 1942, Lord Woolton papers, Bodleian Library, Oxford, ms 2, fol. 153.

2.13 Women and access to food

The following resolution passed by the Women's Co-operative Guild at its 1945 annual conference suggests working-class women were acutely aware of the continuing class differences in access to food.

In view of the cuts in rations which will press with particular hardship upon the working-class, this Congress of the Women's Co-operative Guild calls for the adoption of a points scheme for restaurant meals. We have yet to hear of the wholesale dismissal of chefs employed by the upper classes, whose duty it will now be to cook one shillingsworth of meat, and two pennyworth of corned beef with one ounce of cooking fat per person. We realise that people with money and influence go short of nothing, as there is still unrationed food such as poultry and game, and meals can be obtained in hotels and restaurants. We also protest at the hypocritical propaganda of the BBC and the Press in trying to make us believe that everyone is on the same rations.

Emergency resolution passed at the 1945 Women's Co-operative Guild Annual Congress, in Jean Gaffin and David Thoms, *Caring and Sharing: The Centenary History of the Co-operative Women's Guild*, Manchester, 1983, p. 132.

2.14   A 'monsoon in Mayfair'

Members of the Voluntary Aid Detachments (VADs)[1] were largely drawn from upper-class and upper-middle-class women.

I feel reluctant to address you on a matter so small in the middle of events so large, but the status of some four thousand military V.A.D. Members and their twenty-four Commandants seems likely to provoke a Parliamentary Debate, and if it does, I am anxious that my friends in the Labour Party should know what they are up against.

You will remember that about this time last year an Army Council proposal to merge their V.A.D's in the A.T.S. [Auxiliary Territorial Service[2]] provoked a monsoon in Mayfair.... Anyway,

---

[1] Many members of the VADs were upper- and middle-class women who did basic nursing for the armed forces; as VAD members they were exempt from conscription into less desirable war work, such as in munitions factories.
[2] Women in the ATS were usually employed on clerical and other office work for the army, thereby releasing men for service in fighting units; it lacked the social prestige of the VADs.

it was clear from the start that the V.A.D's had somehow got into a privileged position which the nature of their work and the new conditions of the 'call-up' no longer justified. Their own representatives realised this....

But there has been interminable delay – and now the friends of the V.A.D's (not, I think, their official leaders, and certainly not their former representatives on the Committee) are working up a full-dress political agitation against the agreed scheme, and inviting individual V.A.D's to write to their M.P.'s....

What I particularly want my friends in the Labour Party to realise is this:– the present V.A.D. agitation is a social ramp boiled up by a few influential people on behalf of the wives and daughters of their friends. The V.A.D's themselves ought to be ashamed to make such a fuss about the precise terms on which they will serve their country in war-time. I do hope someone will say this good and hard if the Government allows a Parliamentary discussion. It will be a shocking waste of time and a monstrous concession to social influence if it does.... I do not want to engage in a class war, but I will fight it with the gloves off if this kind of thing goes on.

Mary Stocks (Labour Party supporter and a leader of the Family Endowment Society) to Clement Attlee, 19 July 1943, CAB 118/87, Public Record Office, London.

2.15 Class feeling in the 1945 election

It has been suggested that the overwhelming Labour victory in the 1945 general election reflected the intense class feeling at the end of the war. At least one Conservative candidate, Harold Nicolson, shared that view.

People feel, in a vague and muddled way, that all the sacrifices to which they have been exposed and their separation ... from family life during four or five years, are all the fault of 'them' – namely the authority or the Government. By a totally illogical process of reasoning, they believe that 'they' mean the upper classes, or the Conservatives, and that in some manner all that went well during these five years was due to [Ernest] Bevin and

[Herbert] Morrison, and all that went ill was due to Churchill. Class feeling and class resentment are very strong.

Harold Nicolson to Nigel Nicolson, 27 May 1945, in Nigel Nicolson (ed.), *Harold Nicolson. Diaries and Letters 1939–1945*, London, 1967, p. 465.

2.16   Class feeling at the war's end

> Some people, especially from the middle class, thought class differences became less important during the war, but found that class barriers were revived when the war ended.

When we [the House of Commons factory[3]] were closed down [at the end of the war], although we ended up with a wonderful party and everybody had a fantastic time, the moment the factory was closed all the class barriers raised their ugly heads again. Immediately we were back to surnames and deferential attitudes towards people. Although everybody was congratulating everybody on a wonderful job done, it was quite interesting to see that the barriers remained there and were reinstated the moment the war was over.

Vera Michel-Downes, factory welfare officer, in Joanna Mack and Steve Humphries, *The Making of Modern London 1939–1945: London at War*, London, 1985, p. 169.

---

[3] During the war the cellar underneath the House of Commons was converted into a submarine factory in which House of Commons staff worked during their free time.

3

Race and ethnicity

Prewar patterns of racial and ethnic prejudice continued during the war, and for blacks and Jews probably intensified. This seems inconsistent with the belief that the war created greater social solidarity.

3.1 Attitudes toward Irish workers

Prewar prejudice against the Irish remained so strong during the war that government policies acknowledged it.

Irish labourers were segregated as far as possible and generally they settled down in the peculiar circumstances of the job, remote as they often were, on airfield and other civil engineering contracts, from population centres.... In towns and villages un-used to the ways of life of industrial workers, it was hard enough to find suitable billets for the cleanest and most law-abiding transferees from places in Britain. Generally speaking, house-proud owners of billets found Irish workers even less desirable lodgers. Local authorities responsible under the Ministry of Health for hiring and requisitioning billets looked askance at Irish men and women. Few authorities would agree to the need for compulsory billeting if they suspected vermin and contagious infec-tions, and 'the Ministry of Health had an unwritten but rigid rule that compulsory billeting was never to be used, even as a threat, where Irish workers were concerned, as feelings ran so high'.

A. V. Judges, 'Irish labour in Great Britain, 1939–1945', unpublished official history (civilian), 1948, LAB 8/1528, Public Record Office, London, p. 42.

3.2 'Colour feeling'

After being bombed out of his lodgings in June 1941, Sir Hari Singh Gour, a British citizen, Vice-Chancellor of Nagpur University and a distinguished Indian legal authority, was refused accommodation at the Carnarvon Hotel because he was 'coloured'. As there were many cases like Gour's, and the support of non-Caucasian peoples in the British Empire was crucial to the war effort, some British officials proposed anti-discrimination legislation.

I have long been concerned about colour feeling in this country which is more than ever to be deplored under present conditions when Africans, West Indians and other coloured people throughout the Empire are throwing themselves into our war effort. The answer which you gave [in the House of Commons] on the 19th June on the subject of the Indian case [Sir Hari Singh Gour] shows that you are also anxious to find means of preventing discrimination against British subjects of other races.

From discussions which we have had in the Colonial Office, hotels, whether in possession of liquor licences or otherwise, and public houses are the places where the trouble mainly arises. I am advised that there is a common law obligation on innkeepers to provide accommodation and refreshment for travellers, which can be enforced by a civil action on an indictment, but the obligation is not altogether clear and it has its limitations....

I am wondering whether it would be practicable to pass a statute defining and, if necessary, enlarging this common law right and providing simple means whereby it could be enforced.

So many cases are brought to our notice that there should be little difficulty in bringing prosecutions if the law were defined and simple machinery provided for its enforcement.

Lord Moyne, Colonial Office, to Herbert Morrison (Home Secretary and Minister of Home Security), 27 June 1941, HO 45/24748, Public Record Office, London.

3.3 The problem of black GIs

Faced with an influx of thousands of black GIs, the Secretary of State for War proposed that the British government adopt the policy of racial segregation which the US Army maintained.

1. As my colleagues are aware, the United States authorities are sending to this country the same proportion of coloured troops as obtains generally throughout the United States Army. There are now between 11,000 and 12,000 such troops over here, and this number are likely to be considerably increased. The Secretary for Foreign Affairs ... undertook, with the approval of the War Cabinet, to press the U.S.A. authorities to reduce the number sent over, but I believe has met with little success. We are thus left to face the various problems to which their presence gives rise.

2. The policy of the United States military authorities in dealing with their coloured troops in this country is based on the *modus vivendi* which has been developed in the United States in the course of time as the result of conditions obtaining in that country. Their policy ... rests on the principle of an almost complete separation between white and coloured troops....

3. This policy may perhaps be fairly described as the combination of equal rights and segregation practised in the Southern States and is not generally known to the population of this country, who with little experience of a colour problem at home are naturally inclined to make no distinction between the treatment of white and coloured troops and are apt to regard such distinctions as undemocratic.

4. The War Office is thus faced with two incompatible theories, the disregard of either of which may have serious consequences. On the one hand the average white American soldier does not understand the normal British attitude to the colour problem and his respect for this country may suffer if he sees British troops and British Women's Services drawing no distinction between white and coloured.... Moreover, the coloured troops themselves probably expect to be treated in this country as in the United States, and a markedly different treatment might well cause political difficulties in America at the end of the war. It must be added that from the point of view of the morale of our troops, whether in this country or overseas, it is most undesirable that there should be any unnecessary association between American coloured troops and British women. These considerations suggest that the War Office attitude toward

the American coloured troops should be based on the view of the American Army authorities....

To sum up, I would ask the endorsement of the War Cabinet of the policy I propose to follow in the Army:–

(a) To make full use of the American administrative arrangements for the segregation of coloured troops, but where those fail to make no official discrimination against them.

(b) To give the Army through A.B.C.A. [Army Bureau of Current Affairs] a knowledge of the facts and history of the colour question in the U.S.A. and the U.S.A. Army.

(c) To allow Army officers without the issue of overt or written instructions to interpret those facts to the personnel of the Army including the A.T.S. and so educate them to adopt towards the U.S.A. coloured troops the attitude of the U.S.A. Army Authorities.

War Cabinet memorandum by P. J. Grigg, 'United States coloured troops in the United Kingdom', 3 October 1942, CAB 66/29, WP (42) 441, Public Record Office, London.

3.4 'Avoid becoming too friendly' with blacks

Although officially taking the position that British authorities should not assist the US Army in enforcing segregation, the Cabinet agreed not to object to that policy and to caution Britons against becoming too friendly with black GIs.

(1) There was general agreement that the attitude of the United States Army to this question was a factor of great importance, which must be given due weight in determining the British attitude to coloured American troops.

(2) In particular, it was agreed that it was desirable that the people of the country should avoid becoming too friendly with coloured American troops.

(3) On the other hand, the recommendation at the conclusion of the Secretary of State for War's Memorandum that the personnel of the Army, including A.T.S., should be educated to adopt towards the United States coloured troops the attitude of the United States authorities as at present worded went too far. (The Secretary of State for War agreed that some amendment of

his paper was called for in this respect.) While it was right that our troops and our people should be educated to know what the American attitude was, it was equally important that the Americans should recognise that we had a different problem as regards our coloured people and that a *modus vivendi* between the two points of view should be found.

(4) Turning to the practical issues involved, it was agreed that we need not, and should not, object to the Americans making full use of administrative arrangements for the segregation of their coloured troops. But they must not expect our authorities, civil or military, to assist them in enforcing a policy of segregation.

(5) It was clear that, so far as concerned admission to canteens, public houses, theatres, cinemas, and so forth, there would, and must, be no restriction of the facilities hitherto extended to coloured persons as a result of the arrival of United States troops in the country....

The War Cabinet –

(a) Invited the Lord Privy Seal in consultation with the Home Secretary and the Secretary of State for War, to prepare, in the light of the discussion, a revised memorandum which would be issued as a confidential instruction to Army officers of the rank of Colonel and above as to the guidance in this matter which might be given orally to the troops under their command.

War Cabinet minute, 13 October 1942, CAB 65/28, WM (42) 140, Public Record Office, London.

3.5   Official policy toward black GIs

British service personnel were instructed that they should respect the American attitude toward racial segregation, that it was inappropriate for white women to be alone with black soldiers, and that social gatherings should be segregated.

The coming of American negro troops to this country may place members of the Services in difficult situations owing to the differences of outlook between the white American personnel and the British personnel as to the relationship between black and white people.

It has therefore been thought advisable to issue the following instructions as to the advice which should be given to the British Service personnel in this matter....

It is necessary, therefore, for British men and women to recognise the problem and to take account of the attitude of the white American citizen. This will prevent any straining of our amicable relations with the U.S. Army through misunderstanding which knowledge and forethought can prevent.

2. British soldiers and auxiliaries should try to understand the American attitude to the relationship of white and coloured people, and to appreciate why it is different from the attitude of most people in this country who normally come into contact with only an occasional Negro....

7. There is no reason why British soldiers and auxiliaries should adopt the American attitude but they should respect it and avoid making it a subject for argument and dispute. They must endeavour to understand the American point of view and they must always be on their guard against giving offence.

8. There is certain practical advice which should be given as follows:–

(a) Be friendly and sympathetic towards coloured American troops – but remember that they are not accustomed in their own country to close and intimate relationships with white people.

(b) If you find yourself in the company of white and coloured American troops (as for example if white American troops come into a canteen or bar where you are in the company of coloured Americans) make it your business to avoid unpleasantness. It is much the best, however, to avoid such situations.

(c) For a white woman to go about in the company of a Negro American is likely to lead to controversy and ill-feeling; it may also be misunderstood by the Negro troops themselves. This does not mean that friendly hospitality in the home or in social gatherings need be ruled out, though in such cases care should be taken not to invite white and coloured American troops at the same time.

(d) Avoid arguments over the colour question; but if it happens to come up in discussions with American troops listen patiently to what the Americans have to say and, without necessarily agreeing with them, make up your mind that you will not allow it to become an occasion for ill-feeling or open dispute.

(e) Be on your guard against ill-disposed people who are out to use the colour question as a means of stirring up trouble between the Americans and ourselves.

Memorandum by Stafford Cripps, the Lord Privy Seal, 'United States negro troops in the United Kingdom', 17 October 1942, CAB 66/30, WP (42) 473, Public Record Office, London.

3.6 Anti-discrimination legislation

> After Learie Constantine, a famous West Indian cricket player and British government employee, was refused accommodation by a London hotel because of his race, government officials once again considered legislation against racial discrimination.

Mr. Johns [Ministry of Agriculture] reported on the case of Miss King[1] who cannot be found land army work.... The Ministry [of Agriculture] has experience of the difficulties of placing and billeting with a few other coloured girls, though they were less obviously coloured than Miss King....

Mr. Keith [Colonial Office] said that the question of billeting was a difficulty everywhere for coloured people, and they had experience of this in connection with university students.

Sir Charles Jeffries [Colonial Office] said that, in spite of the difficulties, the Colonial Office was on the whole in favour of legislation prohibiting innkeepers from refusing accommodation on racial grounds. It was considered that such legislation, while of limited practical effect, could be of value in making the attitude of His Majesty's Government clear both to coloured people and to the general public here.

Mr. Gilchrist [India Office] doubted if legislation was the remedy. He said that the number of cases in which Indians were involved was small in view of the many thousands who had been accommodated in this country without undue friction. Unfortunately, for political reasons, much prominence had been given to the few cases where difficulties had been encountered.... The

[1] Amelia King, a third-generation black British citizen, attempted to enlist in the Women's Land Army but was rejected because of her race.

introduction of legislation in this country, he thought, would give undesirable prominence to racialism, which was the exception not the rule, and he thought it would be better to deal with the matter some other way.

Minutes of a meeting convened by the Home Office concerning discrimination in public accommodation, 17 September 1943, HO 45/24748, Public Record Office, London.

3.7 'Coloured' troops and British women

Public unease about sexual relationships between British women and black GIs began to increase during 1943, and the public tended to blame the women involved.

(b) *Coloured troops* (Nine Regions). These are praised. In some cases they are said to be better behaved and 'less sloppy' than the whites; also, in the Huddersfield area, better behaved than the British troops.

People deplore the association of coloured troops with white girls, but it is the latter who are censured. At the same time, it is suggested that the negroes might be provided with a contingent of coloured Auxiliaries, or more camp amenities so that they should spend less time out.

There is some concern at the relations between white and coloured troops and at reports of friction between them. Recent cases of coloured men being condemned to death for rape have aroused strong local protests on grounds of colour discrimination (S.W. Region). In Norwich there is resentment that certain restaurants will not serve negroes.

'United States coloured troops and British women', Home Intelligence report, 8 June 1944, INF 1/292, Public Record Office, London.

3.8 Anti-Semitism

Opinion surveys indicated anti-Semitism increased during the war, even after the existence of the extermination camps in Poland had become public knowledge.

2. *The Jews and Anti-Semitism*
Q: 'Among the people you know, do you think that anti-Jewish feeling is increasing, decreasing, or about the same?'

	Increasing %	Decreasing %	Same %	Don't Know %
Total	25	16	43	16
Total: (Jan. 1942)	19	11	44	26
Men	29	17	42	12
Women	22	14	44	20
Income Groups:				
Higher	32	24	38	6
Middle	29	15	47	9
Lower	24	15	43	18

There is no significant difference in feeling between age groups in the sample.

'The Jews and anti-Semitism', British Institute of Public Opinion survey included in Home Intelligence report, 25 February 1943, INF 1/292, Public Record Office, London.

3.9 The Jews

> Anti-Semitism often took the form of claiming Jews were especially prone to be involved in the black market and in evading conscription.

During the last three weeks comment about Jews in this country appears to have increased slightly. Jews continue to be criticised for black marketing, escaping the call-up and 'displaying ostentatious wealth'.

In London, the North Midland and the North Western Regions, there is said to be an increase in anti-Semitism – 'the spreading of which is seemingly in some cases deliberately organised and fostered'; it is suggested that in Hornsey 'anti-Semitism due to ignorance and prejudice is exploited by Fascist elements'. Reference is also made to 'undue prominence shown in the Press to court cases against Jews'.

'The Jews', Home Intelligence report, 6 May 1943, INF 1/292, Public Record Office, London.

4

Women

The war created new opportunities for women, but it also stimulated a backlash against changes in gender boundaries. Thus, while women were conscripted into war factories and into the women's services, leadership positions were generally reserved for men, and the principle of gendered compensation and employment was upheld. Sexuality, one of the arenas in which unequal power relationships are played out, also became a focal point of wartime gender conflict. The perception that the double standard of sexuality was being undermined increased concern with restricting women's sexual freedom and making marriage and family more appealing.

4.1 Women as policy makers

The uproar following the government's proposal to appoint three men to review the women's services prompted one prominent feminist group, the London and National Society for Women's Service, to suggest that women should be involved in making and administering policy.

I write on behalf of the Executive Committee of the London and National Society for Women's Service with reference to the Government's announcement that they have set up a Committee to report on the standards of amenities and welfare conditions in the three women's Services.

In view of the misgivings on this subject which are known to be widely spread in the community, misgivings which in the view of my Committee have arisen from isolated cases and are not in general justified, we welcome the setting up of an enquiry. We desire, however, to make the following observations:–

1. The successful prosecution of this war depends upon the collaboration of the women in the common effort.

2. The Government is endeavouring to secure the assistance of the women as workers without calling for their assistance in the framing of policies or the direction of schemes of work.

3. In our view this endeavour is in any case obstructive to the attainment of the maximum output, and must, in the case of Services confined entirely to women, inevitably produce the results to be expected from policies framed and schemes directed by inexperienced persons.

These considerations lead us respectfully to beg your attention to the following points:– ...

2. That an entirely male Interdepartmental Committee – even when composed of the Parliamentary Secretaries of the Departments concerned – is not a tribunal to which the people of this country as a whole can look with confidence to deliver judgment upon the working of their own department arrangements for the amenities and welfare of the women in the Services under their authority.

My Committee desire further to express their regret that in view of the present enforced enlistment of women in the National Service, the Government should not have taken the opportunity of the recent changes in the appointment of Ministers to appoint a woman Parliamentary Secretary to the Ministry of Labour. We cannot but see in this omission yet another proof of the Government's reluctance to admit women to share in the counsels which control their destinies, and we would once more urge that if the maximum co-operation of women in the war effort is to be reached they must be given a share in the responsibility no less than the drudgery entailed.

Philippa Strachey (Secretary, London and National Society for Women's Service) to Clement Attlee, 6 February 1942, CAB 118/87, Public Record Office, London.

4.2 War and sexual anxiety

When rumours about sexual immorality in the women's services became so widespread that they hampered recruiting, the government initiated an inquiry. The committee's conclusion that the rumours were without foundation raises a question as to why baseless rumours should have gained widespread acceptance. This may reflect anxiety that women in uniform would adopt male standards of sexual behaviour and a desire to maintain the double standard of sexuality.

199. Virtue has no gossip value....

200. The British ... cherish a deep-rooted prejudice against uniforms; consequently a woman in uniform may rouse a special sense of hostility, conscious and sub-conscious, among certain people who would never give two thoughts to her conduct as a private citizen. The woman in uniform becomes an easy target for gossip and careless talk....

201. War gives rise to many rumours. Vague and discreditable allegations about the conduct of women in the Forces have caused considerable distress and anxiety not only to friends and relations at home but to men fighting overseas. Some of these tales have suggested a high rate of illegitimate pregnancy, others that excessive drinking is a common practice....

202. For the A.T.S., however, we have been supplied with detailed figures on discharges for pregnancy which prove conclusively how little truth there is in the rumour regarding illegitimate pregnancy in that Service. There are in the A.T.S. large numbers of married women and the pregnancies of these women are often, no doubt, carelessly confused with those of single women....

203. Turning to unmarried women, the illegitimate *birth* rate among the age groups from which A.T.S. are recruited is approximately 21.8 per 1,000 per annum. The *pregnancy* rate among single A.T.S. personnel is 15.4 per 1,000 per annum. It must be remembered that pregnancy and birth statistics are not identical, for a woman in the Services – or in any other occupation – discharged for pregnancy may subsequently miscarry.... A number of single women come into the Forces already pregnant. According to the monthly returns for the first five months of this year of single women who were discharged for pregnancy, the percentage who were pregnant before entering the A.T.S. ranged from 18 per cent. to 44 per cent.

204. We can, therefore, with certainty, say that the illegitimate birth rate in the Services is lower than the illegitimate birth rate among the comparable civilian population....

207. We are, however, concerned to point out that the Women's Services, which have now reached a considerable figure, to-day represent a cross section of the population and all types and standards are represented among them. The innocent and the experienced, girls from good and girls from bad homes, are all thrown together. If a woman has learnt loose habits in civilian life, she brings those habits with her into the Services.... Allegations of general immorality in a camp, when investigated, have in our experience, resolved themselves into one or two cases which, in the course of gossip, have been multiplied times over. And the same applies to charges of drunkenness....

We can find no justification for the vague and sweeping charges of immorality which have disturbed public opinion, and in this we are supported by representatives of the various welfare organisations and the Chaplains who are in constant touch with the girls. We have taken careful evidence on this point and find that, in the opinion of those most competent to form a reasoned judgment, promiscuous conduct in the Women's Services is confined to a small proportion of the whole.

'Report of the Committee on Amenities and Welfare Conditions in the Three Women's Services', *Parliamentary Papers 1941–42*, vol. 4, Cmd 6384, London, 1942, pp. 49–51.

4.3 Women and fire-watching

> Male criticism of the government's order requiring women to do fire-watching seemed as concerned about the danger to female virtue as to the possibility of injury from falling bombs.

A feeling of resentment and objection to the Fire-watching order for women is reported this week from four Regions, and is borne out by Postal Censorship; the chief reasons for complaint are that:–

(a) There are thought to be still a lot of men who are avoiding fire-watching duty; women feel that all men should be called upon first. It is suggested that the A.R.P. [Air Raid Precautions] Service and Home Guard, 'who spend long hours of duty doing nothing', and older men up to 65 or 70, should be brought in to fire-watch.

(b) Fire-watching is not a fit job for women; this opinion appears to be held chiefly by men, who are said to be doubtful of women's ability to tackle difficult fires, and dubious 'about the propriety of girls being on duty with men employees at night.'

(c) Fire-watching in target areas should be left to men; women should only fire-watch in residential areas.

'Women's fire-guard order', Home Intelligence report, 27 August 1942, INF 1/292, Public Record Office, London.

4.4 Sex-differentiated compensation

The government's scheme provided higher rates of compensation for war injury to civilian men than to women. The introduction of mandatory fire-watching for women increased support for equal compensation, since women were now being exposed to increased risk of injury.

7. The present political activity on the subject of differentiation in the rates of compensation as between men and women follows the decision to impose compulsory fire prevention duties on women and the agitation is focused on this particular aspect of the problem; but the sex differentiation in rates has been the subject of complaint from time to time, by women Members of Parliament and women's organisations ... and it is obvious that the demands in respect of women fire guards are but an attempted step in the direction of securing Governmental recognition of the principle of equal compensation and eventually equal pay as between men and women....

8. The women's organisations have urged that men and women are on equal terms whilst actually performing fire prevention duties which are unpaid, and that as the conditions and risks are the same, there should be equal compensation. Admittedly, unequal compensation cannot be related directly to a difference in remuneration for these particular duties, but the claim ignores the general inequality of earnings as between men and women, which is relevant, whatever may be the circumstances of the injury, to the measure of compensation to be accorded to those prevented from, or handicapped in, following their normal occupation. What on the face of things appeared equal compensation

would, in effect, be a greater relative degree of compensation to women than to men.

9. But the demand does not, and will not, stop at equal compensation for women fire guards; nor would it be reasonable or just to concede equality of compensation for women fire guards without also extending the principle to women in the Forces and civil defence services, who are at least equally liable to disablement by enemy action. A concession on this scale, however, could not be regarded by the advocates of equal compensation as other than a basis for further demands, e.g., for recognition of the principle of equal pay. Indeed immediately equal compensation for service women, civil defence personnel and fire guards was admitted, the principle of differentiation as regards civilians generally would be threatened and there would inevitably be repercussions on the present sex differentiation in national health insurance and other State schemes. The way would also be cleared for a campaign for equal pay in the Forces, followed by demands for the abolition of sex differentiation among State employees.

'Differentiation of rates of civilian war injury compensation as between men and women', memorandum by Sir Walter Womersley (Minister of Pensions), 25 September 1942, CAB 71/10, LP (42) 215, Public Record Office, London.

4.5 Origin of the Select Committee

Fearing that the government might be defeated if the issue were put to a vote, the Lord President's Committee agreed to an inquiry by a House of Commons Select Committee.

The Committee were informed that about 200 members [MPs] had put their names to this amendment; and Mrs. Tate had indicated that she proposed to press it to a Division. The Labour Party were committed to the principle of equal compensation and in the event of a Division would find it difficult to avoid voting for the Amendment.... In these circumstances it was just possible that the Amendment might be carried against the Government.... To meet this situation the Deputy Prime Minister suggested that the Government should offer to appoint a Committee to consider the questions raised by the Amendment.

In discussion, reference was made to the risk that, if a Committee were now appointed to consider questions involving the principle of equal pay for men and women, there would be dangerous reactions in the discussions which were already proceeding regarding the remuneration of women in industry, particularly the engineering trades. The Minister of Labour and the Minister of Supply felt that, if the Government raised directly at this stage the issue of equal pay, industrial peace might be endangered for the rest of the war. Largely on this account it was felt that the terms of reference of any Committee of enquiry should be confined to the issue of equal compensation, as a war-time problem, and should not embrace the general question of equal pay.

Lord President's Committee minute, 20 November 1942, CAB 71/7, LP (42) 71, Public Record Office, London.

4.6 Sex differentiation and policy

> The government resisted equal compensation because its policies were based on the principle of sex differentiation and would be undermined by the proposed reform.

All we can put from the Treasury point of view, I think, is the general aspect of the question, and I think that amounts to this: The principle of sex differentiation, whether it is right or wrong, is at present a matter of Government policy, and it runs right through a large part of the social structure. It appears in all the social services, with the exception of old age pensions; it appears all through the pay of the Forces, the Civil Defence workers and the Government Service; it is also general in local authority service.... The Government system of salaries in the main is based on the practice outside. The system was laid down in the Tomlin Report on the Civil Service and has been adhered to ever since. It was to the effect that the Government should provide payment and observe conditions which corresponded to the best practice in comparable outside occupations, but it was not contemplated that the Government should run ahead of outside practice, and of course, sex differentiation is deeply embedded in industrial and – though to a slightly less extent – in commercial practice and amongst local authorities; so that when a proposal comes along to depart from this principle in relation to one particular area of State payments or State benefits, we are bound to view it with suspicion, because it is contrary to the general principle on which the vast majority of these payments are based.

Testimony by Sir Alan Barlow, Treasury Department, to the Select Committee on Equal Compensation, 5 January 1943, *Parliamentary Papers, 1942–43*, vol. 3, London, p. 95.

4.7   Equal compensation

The National Council of Women based its case for equal compensation on the ground that all citizens should be treated alike regardless of their gender.

It is the duty of the N.C.W. to watch over the position allotted to women, but they wish to make it plain from the first that while they oppose preferential treatment for men they desire no preferential treatment for women. Their demand is that civilian men and women alike should be treated as citizens fulfilling common duties and sharing common dangers....

We submit that the introduction of sex as a determining factor in compensation for personal injuries is an innovation contrary to precedent, and that the injustice it involves has brought discredit on a scheme which but for this would have been rightly acclaimed as a remarkable achievement on the part of a democracy fighting for its life.

Under the Common Law the right to claim for damages for personal injuries applies equally to gainfully and to non-gainfully occupied persons, and the general damages awarded are based on the pain and suffering of the individual, whether man or woman, special damages being based, equally without regard to sex, on the loss sustained including earnings....

The rights of English women in regard to compensation for personal injuries were therefore equal in the eyes of the law to the rights of English men, until the passing of the Emergency

Provisions [Personal Injuries Act] in September 1939 deprived them of its protection and they were subsequently legislated for under the Ministry of Pensions Schemes as a sex apart....

The National Council of Women respectfully urge the Select Committee ... that compensation to civilians for war injuries should be allocated without regard to the sex of the recipient, and that all citizens should be treated alike by the State.

Memorandum submitted by the National Council of Women to the Select Committee on Equal Compensation, December 1942, *Parliamentary Papers, 1942–43*, vol. 3, appendix J, p. 189.

4.8 Public support for equal compensation

Public opinion backed equal compensation for women, especially after fire-watching became compulsory for them.

Considerable interest has been aroused by the debate on this subject in the House of Commons. Nine Regions report 'a general feeling' that women should be entitled to equal compensation, and 'shock and anger' expressed at the Government having 'won a victory in this matter.'

It is pointed out that 'sending women to target areas does not seem to tally with unequal compensation, to a public that prides itself on fair play', and 'if Parliament won't agree to equal rights now, when women are needed so much, it is not likely that they'll be willing to consider them after the war.'

'Equal compensation for war injuries', Home Intelligence report, 3 December 1942, INF 1/292, Public Record Office, London.

4.9 Equal Citizenship (Blanket) Bill

Rather than addressing each example of sex discrimination separately, the Six Point Group and the Women's Publicity Planning Association attempted to persuade the government to adopt a bill making all forms of sex discrimination illegal.

AN EQUAL CITIZENSHIP (BLANKET) BILL

A bill to abolish sex discrimination in the law and to establish and maintain equality before the law for all citizens without distinctions based on sex.

Explanation

It has been laid down by International Congresses of lawyers from many different countries that a good code of law must apply equally to all citizens alike and must not contain discrimination against any sections of the community on grounds of class, creed, race or sex.

The intention of this Bill is to establish the principle of equal rights and obligations for men and women.

Abolition of Sex Disabilities

Clause I. Henceforth after the passing of this Act, equal rights for men and women shall be recognised as an established principle of law; and, whenever in an Act of Parliament or at Common Law there is any provision which contains a distinction based on sex, it shall be and it is hereby so amended and shall be so interpreted as to admit of no sex discrimination but shall put men and women upon precisely similar footing before the law.

Dorothy Evans, *The Equal Citizenship (Blanket) Bill*, 3rd edn, London, 1944, p. 7.

4.10 Wartime sexuality

> Women experienced greater sexual freedom during the war, but the public viewed it as a form of 'moral delinquency', requiring increased social controls.

During the last two weeks, a good deal of comment and concern have been reported at 'the wave of moral delinquency', chiefly among young people.

Sex: Particular concern is expressed about:

(a) 'Young girls who fling themselves at soldiers'. Some think that, 'with the growing number of enthusiastic amateur prostitutes', the men are not to blame, 'as the girls lie in wait for them on all sides'; but others blame 'the drunken soldiers who are always molesting women and girls'. The need for more women police is the solution most often suggested; others are – a curfew for all young women, or for U.S. troops, and a ban on the sale of alcohol to young women.

(b) The growing number of illegitimate babies, many of coloured men.

(c) The number of wives of men serving abroad who are thought to be associating with U.S. and Dominion troops.

(d) The lack of welfare and supervision for transferred women workers. The unwelcoming attitude of some landladies, together with the small margin of money left for recreation, is blamed for some young girls' readiness to be picked up by soldiers who can give them a good time.

'Morals', Home Intelligence report, 28 October 1943, INF 1/292, Public Record Office, London.

4.11 Women's Land Army and sexuality

Attitudes toward women's increased sexual freedom varied greatly, even among young women.

I read with great interest your remarks on 'War Factory'. I am a land girl [member of Women's Land Army] living in an isolated hostel and I find the same, shall I say, moral decline among our girls here which was noted of women working in factories away from towns. The problem of the land girl strikes me as more important still, as here the girls are younger and less firm in character, away from home for the first time in their lives, doing work which is either very hard and dirty or else deadly monotonous, and they certainly find it hard to interest themselves in it. So all their interests are turned towards their spare time in the evenings. But again, like the factory worker, they care little about mental activities (which is, of course, due to some extent to their physically strenuous day work) and, looking for any kind of entertainment, they find their satisfaction in pub crawling or flirting with soldiers. The girls in my hostel are mostly under twenty and know very well what they are doing, they confess that they had never been drunk before they joined up and that their parents would be very upset could they know of all this 'fun'.

Our work in the Land Army is of great importance to the nation, but sometimes I wonder whether the value of all the tons of corn and potatoes brought in by the girls does balance their really disgusting way of living.... The best reconstruction and security plans won't help us if those for whom they are mainly meant are left to develop into amoral and asocial beings.

Letter to the editor from 'A Land Girl', *New Statesman*, 26, 13 November 1943, p. 317.

4.12   Women and US soldiers

Public concern with sexual relationships between British women and US soldiers increased during the war, and public opinion tended to blame the women.

Reported comment has chiefly centred round:

(a) *Behaviour with women and girls* (Eleven Regions). The whole question, particularly the relationship of young girls with U.S. troops, white and coloured, continues to be widely discussed and to cause much anxiety. *People are critical of*:

(i) *The women and girls concerned* (Ten Regions), who in many cases are said to make most of the running. Blame of the girls is more widespread, and sometimes stronger, than of the men. Their predatoriness is particularly censured; some girls are said to be dunning as many as three or four U.S. soldiers to provide for their coming child. Some people are very concerned at what the Americans are going to say about British girls when they return home. More women police are advocated; satisfaction is expressed where their number has been increased.

'British women and U.S. troops', Home Intelligence report, 8 June 1944, INF 1/292, Public Record Office, London.

4.13   Women in uniform

Uniformed women were perceived as having crossed a gender boundary which entitled men to treat them differently than if they wore 'female' clothing.

Another point which I consider may have escaped their Lord-ships' notice is the fact that the lower deck consider they are entitled to address any Wren in uniform on the grounds that she belongs to their Service. Whilst it is desirable to cultivate good relations between the W.R.N.S. and the Lower Deck, it must be appreciated that in a crowded port with many libertymen ashore who have not seen a white woman for some time,[1] it becomes a matter of embarrassment to be continually addressed by sailors and, not to put it too strongly, to be pestered by requests to accompany them, or to make an appointment for some future date. I am glad to say that on this Station I have personally observed sailors and Wrens 'keeping company' to a considerable extent, but it must be admitted that a considerable percentage of Wren ratings, who are daughters of officers, or of a different social status to men of the Lower Deck, find it most embarrassing to be continually addressed by sailors and even more embarrass-ing to disengage themselves, without causing offence, from such well meaning attempts at making acquaintance. On the other hand, respectable women in plain clothes are rarely addressed by sailors thanks to the natural politeness of the lower deck.

'W. R. N. S. – wearing of plain clothes', memorandum by Admiral P. Somerville (Commander-in-Chief, Eastern Fleet), to the Secretary of the Admiralty, 15 August 1944, ADM 1/15101, Public Record Office, London.

4.14 The future of women munitions workers

Mrs Lewthwaite, interviewed here, began working in a Vickers munitions factory in 1941 doing a job normally performed by a skilled man. Although the wartime labour shortage threatened to undermine the sex segregation of jobs, gender divisions were restored when the war ended.

Would you liked to have stayed in Vickers?
I don't know really. I think we'd had enough by then. We enjoyed all the different jobs, but I don't think it was really a place for girls, no.

[1] WRNS, Women's Royal Naval Service, members of which were called Wrens.

Why?

Because all the lads and men came back from the Forces. We had to go really to let them have their jobs back, you see.

Were you told that or did you just assume it?

No, we were told. We went under those conditions really, that it was just while the war was on. And when they came back of course they had to have their jobs back.

Did any of the girls resent that? Did they feel that it was a bit unfair?

No, I don't think so. Some may have done, but I don't think there was much of that really.

Mrs Lewthwaite, in Elizabeth Roberts, *Women and Families: An Oral History, 1940–1970*, Oxford, 1995, pp. 116–17.

4.15   The Conservative Party and women

The rejection of the following resolution by the Conservative Party at its 1945 conference reflects a concern to prevent wartime changes in women's roles from continuing into the postwar period.

That with the object of maintaining in the peace the partnership between men and women as full citizens that has proved so successful in war, this Conference affirms its belief that it is in the interest of the nation that opportunities and rewards shall be open equally to both sexes in order to ensure that the best mind or hand shall have the same chance to excel.

National Union of Conservative and Unionist Associations, *Notes on Current Politics*, April 1945, p. 14.

5

The family

Wartime family life does not seem consistent with the model of increased social solidarity. The war disrupted family life, increasing tensions between parents and children and between spouses. Evacuation separated children from parents, while military service meant that families were often fatherless and husbandless for much of the war. Rising divorce and juvenile delinquency rates suggest the increased stress imposed on the family. The number of persons found guilty of cruelty to or neglect of children rose each year after 1940; by the end of the war the number had more than doubled from the 1940 level.

5.1 Evacuation and the family

Although the Dunkirk spirit is claimed to have encouraged a sense of social solidarity, this is not always apparent in the reports on evacuees.

(d) *Evacuation.* On the basis of many reports ... the situation may be summarised as follows:–

1. In spite of some of the complications produced by voluntary refugees, the Government evacuees were at first well received – far better than last year; hosts felt that the evacuees were this time in genuine need. In many areas, however, certain well-to-do people would not take in evacuees, and compulsory billeting had to be resorted to. The authorities were often reluctant to do this as the unco-operative people were usually of some influence locally....

2. Friction between hosts and evacuees is now rapidly growing for several reasons:–
   a. social incompatibilities.
   b. the use of one kitchen by two or more women.

c. the unco-operative attitude of hosts, and the untidy and dirty habits of evacuees.

d. over-crowding.

e. the splitting up of families.

f. lack of occupation for evacuee women.

All of these factors, especially the last, helped to make the first evacuation a failure, and there is a great danger that the same thing may happen again. This is particularly stressed by the experienced social workers.

'Evacuation', Home Intelligence report, 28 October – 4 November 1940, INF 1/292, Public Record Office, London.

5.2   Effects of evacuation on children

As a result of being separated from their parents for an extended period, some children became more independent and self-reliant. Mrs Wheaton was seven years old when she was evacuated from her home for ten months.

I can realize now that I never turned to my parents for help or anything at all after I came back [from being evacuated]; and looking at my life, what I can remember of it before I went away, I wasn't like that when I came back. If I had problems at school, I sorted them out myself. In fact, I attacked a boy who had previously bullied me. I grabbed him by the scruff of the neck and got him against the wall and he was crying and that was the end of them. They never bullied me after that.

Mrs Wheaton, in Elizabeth Roberts, *Women and Families: An Oral History, 1940–1970*, Oxford, 1995, p. 47.

5.3   Juveniles

During the war there was considerable concern about the effect of weakened family ties on juveniles.

A considerable increase in juvenile crime is causing concern in many districts; the explanation given is generally the slackening of parental control, coupled with the unsettling effect of unprecedented high wages, which are now being paid to boys who take the place of men.... It is thought by social workers that lack of any incentive to save, plus the fact that there are few reasonable pleasures on which to spend this 'easy money', must create serious danger for young people, at a time when violence and destruction on a vast scale are inevitably held up as an admirable human activity.

A Liverpool schoolmaster alleges that in the city there are at least 200 'cellar clubs' where boys and girls indulge in 'an orgy of gambling and drinking'.

'Juveniles', Home Intelligence report, 2–9 July 1941, INF 1/292, Public Record Office, London.

5.4 Problems of youth

Reports such as the following contributed to the perception that the family was breaking down and would need to be 'rebuilt' after the war.

During the past seven weeks, ten Regional reports have referred (most of them more than once) to the behaviour of young people. Public concern is increasing about:

(a) *The growth of juvenile delinquency.* 'Children and young people don't seem to know right from wrong.'

The present methods of treatment are considered inadequate: 'The position needs serious consideration and careful and sympathetic investigation'. In Wales, 'calls are made' for younger magistrates and for teacher magistrates.

(b) *The unruliness and destructiveness* of children and youths. Particular mention is made of their destruction of produce in allotments, and of bombed property. Instances are also given:

(i) From Isleworth, of 'small boys who started fires which gutted a church, the police-station, and two fire-stations';

(ii) From Battle, of boys who 'slashed and tore a marquee especially erected for the feeding of troops, and broke up the tables inside'.

(c) *The immorality of young girls*, particularly those in their early 'teens. Stories are reported from the Eastern Region of 'innumerable girls being pregnant by U.S. soldiers, whether black or white'; and in the North Midland Region the conduct of young girls with black troops is felt to call for better surveillance.

(d) *Excessive drinking* by lads and young girls, 'the girls being tempted by the Forces'.

'Youth', Home Intelligence report, 15 July 1943, INF 1/292, Public Record Office, London.

5.5 Youth

As public concern about juvenile behaviour increased, mothers were often singled out for blame.

During the past four weeks comment has again been on familiar lines. There has been some increase in the volume of complaints, however, – particularly of the immorality of young girls (Ten Regions as compared with seven last month), and the behaviour of children (Seven Regions as compared with four last month). There is particular concern about the damaging of property (Five Regions): breaking of windows, slashing cinema seats, smashing electric light bulbs in trains, and damage to parks and gardens are all alleged.

Factors blamed are:

(a) *Lack of parental control* (Seven Regions) particularly where mothers are at work (Four Regions). Women, it is suggested, should not be allowed to take full-time jobs unless they are able to satisfy the authorities that their children will be looked after in their absence.

(b) *The irresponsibility of parents* (Four Regions) particularly of working mothers 'with money to spare' who spend their time in pubs and cinemas.

'Youth', Home Intelligence report, 2 June 1944, INF 1/292, Public Record Office, London.

5.6 The Blackwell case

Wives who had assumed that any money they saved from their housekeeping allowance was their property were shocked by an appeal court ruling in the Blackwell case. It was a dramatic reminder that wives were financially dependent on their husbands and stimulated movements to reform the law.

On 28th October the Court of Appeal decided against the appeal by Mrs. Dorothy Ursula Blackwell for the reversal of the recent decision by the Oxford County Court that a sum of £103 10s., standing to her credit with the Oxford and District Co-operative Society, was not her property but that of her husband from whom she was separated in 1941. It was not disputed that this money represented her savings out of her housekeeping allowance and the profit she made by taking in lodgers from 1936 onwards....

Lord Justice Goddard suggested that she might let her husband go short of food while she 'built up a bank account'. Facetiously, he pictured her giving him corned instead of roast beef for dinner. It would, he said, be 'a dreadful thing' to hold that her savings were her own; it would tempt husbands to stint their wives.... Lord Justice Goddard opined that even if a married couple agreed that the savings out of the housekeeping money should be the wife's such agreement would not necessarily constitute a legal contract....

Dismissing the appeal, Lord Justice Scott said: 'There is no justification at all for the contention that where a husband hands to his wife an allowance for housekeeping purposes, the husband is to be taken, as a matter of law, as presenting savings out of that money to the wife for her sole use'.... Meantime Dr. [Edith] Summerskill, supported by 43 other M.P.s, has tabled a motion calling for the amendment of the Married Women's Property Act, 1882, to secure to married women a legal right to reasonable savings from their housekeeping allowance.

'Blackwell case', *The Catholic Citizen*, 15 November 1943, p. 58.

5.7 Married women's savings

The Blackwell case stimulated much public criticism, in part because of the inconsistency between the wife's subordinate legal position and the wartime reality that,

with their husbands away in the services, wives functioned
as the head of their families.

Criticism of the recent decision that money saved on housekeeping is the property of the husband comes from seven Regions.
Many people, particularly women, are indignant, strongly
condemning the 'antiquated law', but there is also some amused
comment. According to men, wise housewives do not support the
paying of a wage by a husband, as this would jeopardise the
comradeship of married life.

'Married women's savings', Home Intelligence report, 11 November
1943, INF 1/292, Public Record Office, London.

5.8 Spousal relations

Wives were forced to assume greater responsibility within
the family during the war, and for some this led to a desire
for shared authority and a companionate marriage.

I suddenly thought tonight, 'I know why a lot of women have
gone into pants – it's a sign that they are asserting themselves in
some way.' I feel pants are more a sign of the times than I
realised. A growing contempt for man in general creeps over me.
For a craftsman, whether a sweep or Prime Minister – 'hats off'.
But why this 'Lords of Creation' attitude on men's part? I'm
beginning to see I'm a really clever woman in my own line, and
not the 'odd' or 'uneducated' woman that I've had dinned into
me. Not that in-laws have bothered me for some time now. I got
on my top note, and swept all clean, after one sticky bit of
interference and bother. I feel that, in the world of tomorrow,
marriage will be – will *have* to be – more of a partnership, less of
this '*I* have spoken' attitude. They will talk things over – talking
does do good, if only to clear the air. I run my house like a
business: I have had to, to get all done properly, everything fitted
in. Why, then, should women not be looked on as partners, as
'business women'?

Nella Last's diary entry for 1 August 1943, in Richard Broad and Suzie
Fleming (eds), *Nella Last's War*, London, 1983, pp. 254–6.

80

5.9   Wives and sexuality

> Although servicemen's sexual activity was condoned, their
> wives were expected to remain celibate. This double
> standard of sexuality became a subject of public debate
> when a serviceman killed his wife after discovering she had
> become pregnant by another man and the judge released
> him without penalty.

There can be few of us who have not felt considerably irritated by
the one-sided outlook portrayed in the spate of heartbreak articles
which have appeared lately on the unhappy plight of service men
returning home to discover their wives have been sexually
unfaithful. Whether mere physical satisfaction, sought while a
loved partner is forced to be absent for years at a time should be
called unfaithfulness is a debateable subject. In the past it was a
debateable point whether there should be licence in sexual
matters.

THIS IS NO LONGER SO! The War Office, in allowing the
free issue of contraceptives to men serving abroad, whether
married or single, has adopted the principle that married men
must be free in these matters. We civilians have acquiesced in the
adoption of this principle in that we have not raised our voices
against it. We have not even insisted that the issue of contraceptives should only be made to men whose wives are agreeable.
There has been no suggestion of issuing contraceptives to wives,
who have had to adjust themselves to living without their service
husbands for four or five years or longer.

WHY THIS DIFFERENCE? The sudden cessation of their sex
life has been as unendurable a privation to these women as their
partners. These women, in facing the hardships of life on the
Home Front have been warriors no less courageous than their
men serving abroad. Not only have men and women failed to
admit and recognize that a woman's sexual needs are as urgent as
a man's, but the pendulum has swung as sharply as ever in the
opposite direction, giving the male partner in marriage greater
freedom and at the same time attempting to tie the woman more
closely. The most biting example of this was shown in the recent
acquittal of a young man charged with strangling his wife in
Nottingham Hospital on the grounds, claimed by the Justice, that
the provocation under which the act was committed (the wife's

admission that her pregnancy was due to association with another soldier and her refusal to give the man's name) was such that any man would have committed it in the circumstances.

To man has been assigned the right and protection to satisfy his sexual needs as and how he may please.

To woman is denied this right and if she tries to exercise it she may be murdered, *together with her unborn child* and society is to be asked to wink at the slaughter.

Are we to slip back to the principles of the so-called Dark Ages or shall we go forward?

Dorothy Wilson, letter to the editor, *Wife and Citizen*, August 1945, p. 31.

5.10 Wards of the state

> A letter to a national newspaper by Lady Allen triggered intense public debate and a committee of inquiry into the treatment of children who were wards of the state or of a charitable organisation. The Report of the Curtis Committee (Care of Children Committee) provided the basis for the 1948 Children Act.

Thoughtful consideration is being given to many fundamental problems, but in reconstruction plans one section of the community has, so far, been entirely forgotten.

I write of those children who, because of their family misfortune, find themselves under the guardianship of a Government department or one of the many charitable organizations. The public are, for the most part, unaware that many thousands of these children are being brought up under repressive conditions that are generations out of date and are unworthy of our traditional care for children. Many who are orphaned, destitute, or neglected still live under the chill stigma of 'charity'; too often they form groups isolated from the main stream of life and education, and few of them know the comfort and security of individual affection. A letter does not allow space for detailed evidence.

In many 'Homes', both charitable and public, the willing staff are, for the most part, overworked, underpaid, and untrained;

indeed there is no recognized system of training. Inspection, for which the Ministry of Health, the Home Office, or the Board of Education may be nominally responsible, is totally inadequate, and few standards are established or expected. Because no one Government department is fully responsible, the problem is the more difficult to tackle.

A public inquiry, with full Government support, is urgently needed to explore this largely uncivilized territory. Its mandate should be to ascertain whether the public and charitable organizations are, in fact, enabling these children to lead full and happy lives and to make recommendations how the community can compensate them for the family life they have lost. In particular, the inquiry should investigate what arrangements can be made (by regional reception centres or in other ways) for the careful consideration of the individual children before they are finally placed with foster-parents or otherwise provided for; how the use of large residential homes can be avoided; how staff can be appropriately trained and ensured adequate salaries and suitable conditions of work, and how central administrative responsibility can best be secured so that standards can be set and can be maintained by adequate inspection.

The social upheaval caused by the war has not only increased this army of unhappy children, but presents the opportunity for transforming the conditions.

Marjory Allen of Hurtwood, letter to the editor, *The Times*, 15 July 1944, quoted in Marjory Allen and Mary Nicholson, *Memoirs of an Uneducated Lady: Lady Allen of Hurtwood*, London, 1975, pp. 178–9.

5.11   Children in foster care

The death of thirteen-year-old Dennis O'Neill in January 1945 as a result of mistreatment by his foster parents focused attention on the nearly 125,000 children for whom local authorities were responsible. The case strengthened public pressure for an inquiry into the care of children deprived of a normal home life.

A story of alleged cruelty to a boy of 13 by his foster-parents was told by counsel at Pontesbury, near Shrewsbury, yesterday, when

Reginald Gough (31), a farmer ... and his wife Esther (29) were both charged with the manslaughter of Dennis O'Neill....

On May 30, 1940, Newport Juvenile Court committed the boy and his two brothers Terence, aged 9, and a younger boy, Frederick, to the care of Newport Council on the ground they were in need of care and attention, their parents having been previously convicted of offences against them. From 1940 until June, 1944, they were in the care of other people. At the end of June last [1944] Gough signed an undertaking that he would care for Dennis....

On January 9 Mrs. Gough rang up Dr. Davies and said that Dennis was in a fit. When the doctor arrived he found him lying dead in a room in a shocking condition....

[Mr H. H. Maddocks, who appeared for the prosecution, said:] 'He was undernourished and practically starved. No fat was found on him, and you will see pictures ... showing signs on his back that he had been unmercifully beaten and signs on his chest where he had been assaulted....

'The pathologist is of the opinion that the actual cause of death was probably the assault which caused the chest injuries, the boy being at that time in an emaciated and weak state of health...'.

According to Terence, their food consisted chiefly of three pieces of bread and butter and tea.... The boys used to go into the pantry and take a bite at anything they could find, and Terence says they were usually discovered and unmercifully beaten....

[On the night before his death] Dennis's feet were in a terrible condition and Gough tried three or four times to make him stop crying. The last time Gough went to him he put his knee on the bed and banged Dennis with his fist on his chest. The boy was in terrible pain and cried out, 'Oh, my back, my back!'

Manchester Guardian, 13 February 1945, p. 2.

5.12   What to do about poor parenting?

By the end of the war the plight of children suffering from parental cruelty or neglect had become a matter of considerable concern. While convinced that it was an important problem, authorities were unclear as to how to ensure good parenting.

Last week's debate in the House of Lords on the problem of homeless and neglected children did not make any very helpful contribution toward a solution.... There was a plea from Lord Denham for the flogging of parents convicted of cruelty....

Perhaps the most realistic speech was made by the Bishop of Sheffield, who suggested that the problem was not so much one of neglected children as of negligent and cruel parents, and that while the short-term policy should aim at rescuing the children, in the long-term it has to be decided what should be done with the parents. Sentencing the parents to terms of imprisonment – or to flogging – solves nothing so far as the children are concerned. In fact, their fate, if they are to be returned to their parents after such punishment, may well be worse. It was recently announced that the Bath magistrates, with the approval of the Home Office, had sentenced a mother, convicted of neglecting her four-year-old child, to a term of compulsory training in parent craft, at the end of which, if she had benefited from it, her child would be returned to her. For the present it may well be impossible for such a punishment to be meted out in more than a few cases of neglect. But it is a policy worth working for.

'Neglected children', *The Economist*, 148, 7 April 1945, p. 443.

6

Crime

The belief that Dunkirk created a new sense of social solidarity does not seem consistent with the increased crime and juvenile delinquency rates in 1940 and in the following years. Magistrates were so alarmed by this trend that they resorted to more severe punishments in an attempt to stem the tide of increased criminal activity. As Mannheim notes in document 6.4, the higher crime rate was not due to professional criminals taking advantage of the war, but to normally law-abiding citizens breaking the law.

6.1 Looting

Looting began to be a serious problem in 1940, only a few months after the evacuation at Dunkirk.

There have been many cases of looting which though not of the gravest kind must be regarded seriously. Damage to premises, including the shattering of windows, has led to the exposure of a great deal of valuable property, and the police are finding much difficulty in providing adequate measures of protection, especially during the hours of black-out. The temptation to take exposed goods is very great and unless drastic penalties are imposed there is substantial danger that the practice may become still more widespread. Representations have been made to me from various quarters as to the need for doing everything possible to protect those who have been injured by enemy action from suffering still further injury owing to the looting of their possessions.... I am told that the imposition of long sentences in certain cases has already had some deterrent effect, but looting is still a serious problem.

Herbert Morrison (Home Secretary) to Winston Churchill, 10 December 1940, PREM 4/40/19, Public Record Office, London.

6.2   Sentences for looting too severe?

Concerned about the manpower shortage, the Prime
Minister attempted to pressure the Home Secretary into
reducing the sentences of six London firemen sentenced to
five-year prison terms for looting.

Perhaps you will very kindly let me know what your final
decision is. They were terrible sentences and we have none too
many able-bodied men.

Winston Churchill to Herbert Morrison, 5 April 1941, PREM 4/40/19,
Public Record Office, London.

6.3   Sentences for looting

Although he promised a review of sentences imposed on
looters, the Home Secretary considered the need to deter
potential looters sufficiently serious for him to refuse to
succumb to the Prime Minister's pressure for lighter
sentences.

I have now had before me full reports on the cases of the six
firemen who were sentenced to five years' penal servitude for
looting.

It seems clear that the offences of which they were convicted
were no worse than those for which many other men have
received lighter sentences. Examination of a large number of
cases which have been reported in the Press shows that sentences
covering a very wide range have been passed for apparently
similar offences not only on soldiers, firemen, policemen, and
other men in positions of trust but also on ordinary civilians; and
there has without doubt been much inequality of punishment. As
I explained, however, in my minute of 10th December last, I have
no power to secure uniformity of sentences.

The cases of these firemen will certainly be included in the
review of the severe sentences on looters which, as I have stated
in my previous minute, I propose to undertake in due course....
While it is true that looting does not seem to be greatly on the
increase at present, it is still far too prevalent, and may well

become worse at any moment with the intensification of bombing. The present cases could not be dealt with apart from a number of others, and in any event we cannot, in my opinion, afford to give any impression that the Government take a more lenient view of looting than the Courts.

Herbert Morrison to Winston Churchill, 20 May 1941, PREM 4/40/19, Public Record Office, London.

6.4   Wartime crime

Hermann Mannheim was lecturer in criminology at the London School of Economics and Political Science during the war, and author of several important wartime studies of the war's effect on crime.

LOOTING

Certainly not the most important but at least the most spectacular criminological feature of the war has been the advent of looting as a result of air raids.

According to The Defence (General) Regulations, 1939, No. 38A, this offence can be committed 'in an area which has been subjected to attack by the enemy ... or in any area to which this Regulation has been applied by order of the Minister of Home Security'; and it implies, apart from other less important cases, stealing from premises damaged by war operations or vacated by reason of attack by the enemy, or stealing articles which have been left exposed or unprotected as a consequence of war operations. The maximum penalty for looting is death or penal servitude for life, and, by Order in Council of October 4, 1940, courts of summary jurisdiction have been given power to impose sentences of imprisonment up to twelve months, instead of the previous maximum of three months.

Looting cases began to come before the London courts very soon after the first air raids. In September 1940 there were 539 cases, in October 1,662, in November 1,463, and in December 920 cases in the Metropolitan Area alone, and a special Anti-Loot Squad of detectives had to be formed by Scotland Yard. At the beginning of February 1941 a gas company inspector stated at a London juvenile court that there had been more than three thousand cases of thefts from [coin-operated] gas meters, mainly in bombed houses. At Leeds Assizes in March 1941, the judge, referring to a 'perfect outburst of looting' at Sheffield after the raids in December 1940, dealt with seventeen charges of looting.

In the Metropolitan Area, 14 per cent of the offenders were schoolboys, and 45 per cent were under 21.... Among 228 looting cases, collected by the author from newspaper reports, with the assistance of the Howard League for Penal Reform, it was found that 211 had no known previous convictions. Although it is too early to make any definite statement, the old experience seems to be confirmed that in times of war the percentage of first offenders tends to increase. The offenders belonged to the following age groups:

Under 17:　6
17–21:　　7
21–30:　 20
30–40:　 73
40–50:　 27
Over 50:　20
Rest unknown

It thus appears that most cases of juveniles have not been reported in the press. No fewer than 95 looters, i.e. 42 percent, were in official positions or at least in positions of trust as air raid wardens, auxiliary firemen or policemen, A.R.P. demolition or rescue workers, and so forth....

ATTITUDES TOWARD LOOTING

Most interesting has been the reaction of the courts and the public toward this new type of crime. As might be expected, the matter has become a favourite topic in the press, where the courts have often been strongly blamed for being either too lenient or too severe....

1. During the first stage, lasting approximately until the middle of October 1940, magistrates, though almost invariably referring to the possibility of a death sentence, as a rule confined themselves to fines or short prison sentences. For this they came in for a lot of criticism, especially as looting cases were increasing during October.

2. As a consequence, police courts resorted to more drastic measures, especially against men in official or semi-official

positions. They were usually committed to assizes, where heavy sentences of penal servitude became not uncommon.

PROFITEERING

There may be still another reason why the public and the courts are beginning to feel somewhat uneasy at the imposition of harsh penalties for looting. It is the growing extent of profiteering in foodstuffs and other commodities – a menace which is slowly being recognized as no less serious than looting. 'They do not steal and they would call themselves traders or businessmen, but they are looters none the less'.

No statistics have as yet been published which would show the actual frequency of such offences. The figures are included in the 'prosecutions under the food control orders,' of which 17,319 were successfully undertaken by the Ministry of Food between the outbreak of the war and the end of April 1941. There are now over two thousand such cases before the courts every month.

Whereas previously not much was said about it in public, the matter has become front-page news since the beginning of May 1941, when a strongly worded statement was published by the Food Price Committee, North Midland Region, to the effect that 'speculation is rampant,' that 'people who render no service in distribution are enriching themselves at the expense of the consumer,' that 'prices have in consequence risen out of all reasonable proportion,' and that the trivial fines imposed by some benches were 'a matter of ridicule.'

Hermann Mannheim, 'Crime in wartime England', *Annals of the American Academy of Political and Social Science*, 217, September 1941, pp. 134–6.

6.5 The black market

Although it is impossible to document the extent of the wartime black market, it appears to have been widespread, with a highly organised distribution system.

A year ago Lord Woolton, Minister of Food, made a speech in which he promised that the Black Market would be driven out of business. In the intervening period the Black Market has grown from a small individual 'racket' into an enormous highly-efficient and totally unscrupulous organisation. Now Parliament has discussed repressive measures. So much for speeches.

Lord Woolton, one of the very few men whose Ministry has been a success, undoubtedly did his best. The Ministry of Food undertook a vast number of prosecutions, but fines mean nothing to gentry who are making enormous profits. Furthermore, these prosecutions touched only the fringe of the market. All these men with the interesting names who have been fined, and in a few cases sentenced to a month or so in prison, are the servants. The big men in business have not been touched and the big men do not object to fines at all and are not moved by prison sentences that do not touch them personally. Make no mistake about it. There are big men at the back of the Black Market; there is a big distributive organisation; there is a big warehousing organisation; there is a highly effective intelligence service. The Black Market is not made up of a large number of individuals acting independently, but a large number of individuals well organised. The thefts are on too large a scale for it to be otherwise. You cannot store 40 thousand eggs nor 5 tons of meat on the kitchen shelves. And these quantities are not easy to distribute.

The Field, March 1942, reprinted in Sadie Ward, *War in the Countryside 1939–45*, London, 1988, p. 76.

6.6   The Hereford case

> During 1941 and 1942 magistrates increasingly ordered juvenile offenders to be birched, in an attempt to stem the rise in juvenile crime. The Hereford case was a turning point because it drew attention to the incompatibility of birching with the right of appeal.

1. On 12th January, 1943 two boys, William James Payne, aged 13, and Dennis Harold Craddock, aged 11, appeared before the Juvenile Court for the City of Hereford to answer two summonses preferred against them by Chief Inspector Wheatley of the Hereford City Police. The first charged them with breaking and entering St. Martin's School between 19th and 20th December,

1942 and stealing therein a number of crayons, pencils and other things to the value 12s. 6d. The second charged them, ... with breaking and entering on 1st January, 1943, a store at a hostel and stealing therein a considerable amount of goods to the value of £35 14s. 0d.... On 26th January the adjourned hearing took place and each boy was sentenced to receive 4 strokes with a birch rod on the charge of malicious damage, and on the charges of larceny, the charges of breaking and entering having been withdrawn, they were committed to the care of the Local Education Authority until they were 18 years of age....

It is no part of my duty to express any opinion on the sentence or any part of it beyond saying that it was one which it was within their discretion lawfully to impose.... It would also be desirable, to prevent any possibility of mistake, that in future, if corporal punishment is awarded by the Court, a direct question should be put to the parents if present, whether they desire to witness the birching or not. I have already ventured to express the opinion that the wording of the Statute creates a difficulty regarding the carrying out of a sentence of corporal punishment while there is a possibility of appeal. It is not easy to envisage a remedy short of suspending the birching till the time for appealing has expired, a course which would not be regarded as in the interests of the child.

'Hereford juvenile court inquiry', *Parliamentary Papers 1942–43*, vol. 4, Cmd 6485, London, 1943, pp. 1, 18.

6.7   Punishment by birching

The public outcry against the use of corporal punishment following the Hereford incident led to demands that the law be amended to deny magistrates the power to order it. The Home Secretary, however, chose instead to caution magistrates against it.

The question whether the courts should by an amendment of the law be deprived of power to order birching is ... controversial; but in the memorandum on Juvenile Offences sent to justices in June, 1941, they were reminded:

'that the Departmental Committee on Corporal Punishment came unanimously to the conclusion that, as a court penalty, corporal punishment is not a suitable or effective remedy for dealing with young offenders'.

Herbert Morrison, *Hansard, Parliamentary Debates*, fifth series, vol. 393, 4 November 1943, c. 847.

6.8   The Hereford case and birching

The Hereford case stimulated considerable public comment on the appropriateness of birching, and much public criticism of local magistrates.

Juvenile Courts
The Hereford Case still causes much discussion, particularly:

(a) *The excessive publicity* (Six Regions). This is already said to have stirred up virulent personal talk directed quite unfairly at local magistrates (South Western Region).

(b) *The pros and cons of birching* (Six Regions). The Scottish report says that the majority are against birching, and that widespread indignation has been caused by the statement of the Chief Constable of Renfrewshire that he would 'use a green birch and cut them with it'. Nevertheless many upholders of corporal punishment are to be found (Four Regions); they feel that young delinquents should be dealt with firmly and that birching may be the only way of dealing with the worst.

'Juvenile courts', Home Intelligence report, 18 November 1943, INF 1/292, Public Record Office, London.

6.9   Juvenile delinquency

By 1943 the problem of juvenile delinquency had become a recurring theme in Home Intelligence reports.

(b) *Juvenile delinquency and hooliganism* (Nine Regions). Wanton damage to property and unruly 'gangs' in the streets are deplored. Lack of parental control (Four Regions), high wages, and the films are blamed. It is suggested that the Hereford Court

Case gave undesirable publicity to the only form of correction which might act as a deterrent.

Youth Organisations are praised (Six Regions) and it is hoped they will be extended. A new interest in them is thought to exist; some who were formerly against compulsory membership of youth organisations are now veering round to the view that this is the only way to check juvenile delinquency.

'Juvenile delinquency', Home Intelligence report, 16 December 1943, INF 1/292, Public Record Office, London.

6.10   Punishing the juvenile

Despite the public support for birching, the Home Office maintained its prewar position that it was an ineffective deterrent which should be abandoned.

9. *Birching*

It was no doubt the desire for some short sharp penalty which led to an unfortunate tendency in some quarters to revert to birching. The advocates of birching seem to think that the objections to it are based on sloppy sentimentality and are disproved by their own experiences during their robust schooldays. Both of these are entirely false notions. As explained in paragraph 22 of the Memorandum issued in June, 1941, the Departmental Committee on Corporal Punishment recommended the abolition of birching as a court penalty on evidence that the most experienced Juvenile Courts had abandoned it after finding that it was not an efficacious deterrent and was apt to do more harm than good. The Committee drew attention to the obvious differences between a caning administered by a parent or schoolmaster and following quickly on a child's misdeed and a birching ordered by the Court after the delays which are essential if proper enquiry is made.

The number of birchings in recent years has been as follows:–

1939	58
1940	307
1941	546
1942	321
1943	167
1944	37

The Hereford case no doubt helped in the reduction which has taken place since 1941, but the reduction had started before that case received publicity and it is probable that birching has again been found to be ineffective as a deterrent.

Memorandum by D. M. G. (a Home Office official), 'Juvenile delinquency', August 1945, CAB 102/790, Public Record Office, London.

7

Public opinion

Before the war, the government had anticipated enemy bombing raids would result in widespread nervous breakdown and hysteria among the public. When this did not occur, 'the negative fact that British morale had not collapsed under bombing was transformed into the positive myth that everyone had acted heroically'.[1] As the following selections suggest, there was considerable variation in civilian response to the Blitz. While there were heroic individuals, the image of the cheerful cockney owes much to the government's desire to keep public morale high and to bring the United States into the war.[2]

7.1 London in the Blitz

Home Intelligence and Mass-Observation reports are not entirely consistent with the claim that Dunkirk created a sense of social unity.

People cheerful and optimistic at weekend when Hitler failed to invade Britain on Friday as threatened. General feeling now that war will last a long time, as invasion cannot succeed and we shall then settle down to hammering away at Germany by R.A.F. [Royal Air Force]. Strong resentment still felt among all classes at Silent Column Campaign and at police prosecutions for spreading rumour, which are considered 'ridiculous'. M.O.I. [Ministry of Information] becoming unpopular again; much of this feeling directed against the Minister. Indignation expressed at what people say to be 'a policy which is turning us into a nation of spies'. Labour Party Candidates' meeting agreed that prosecutions

---

[1] Angus Calder, 'Foreword', in Pete Grafton (ed.), *You, You and You! The People Out of Step with World War II*, London, 1981.
[2] Nicholas John Cull, *Selling War: The British Propaganda Campaign Against American 'Neutrality' in World War II*, Oxford, 1995, p. 98.

for idle talking were upsetting public morale seriously. People in new positions of minor authority accused of officiousness and bullying manner, reminiscent some say 'of the early days of the Nazis'.... Most coloured people reported anxious to pull weight in war effort; unable to, except in St. Pancras where twenty are A.R.P. wardens. Some dismissals because of colour.

'London', Home Intelligence report, 22 July 1940, INF 1/264, Public Record Office, London.

7.2 Morale in Coventry

During the night of 14 November 1940, Coventry city centre was almost completely destroyed by enemy bombs. Coventry police estimated that in the following weeks nearly 100,000 people – about one-half the population – left the city each night, but returned the following morning.

1) The shock effect was greater in Coventry than in the East End or any other bombed area previously studied. This was partly due to the concentrated nature of the damage and to extreme dislocation of services, partly to the small size of the town which meant that many people were directly or indirectly involved. The considerable proportion of imported labour and the fact that Coventry was economically flourishing contributed to this effect.

2) During Friday there was great depression, a widespread feeling of impotence and many open sign [*sic*] of hysteria. 'This is the end of Coventry' expressed the general feeling. Many people tried to leave the city before darkness fell. A quiet night followed by a fine morning changed the atmosphere for the better.

3) There was very little grumbling even about the inadequacies of shelters and in the town itself observers found no anti-war feeling. There was little recrimination or blame.

'Special report on Coventry', Home Intelligence report, 19 November 1940, INF 1/292, Public Record Office, London.

7.3 Portsmouth under attack

The bombing raids had an especially severe effect on public morale in Portsmouth.

On all sides we heard that looting and wanton destruction had reached alarming proportions. The police seem unable to exercise control and we heard many tales of the wreckage of shelters and of stealing from damaged houses, and were told that some people were afraid to take shelter in an attack for fear of being robbed of their remaining possessions. This seems another illustration of the lack of community spirit. The effect on morale is bad and there is a general feeling of desperation as there seems to be no solution. Some of the trouble is caused by children, many of whom do not go to school, though attendance for half a day is again compulsory, but the worst offenders appear to be youths of 18 or 19, though it is difficult to judge as few are caught.

The morale of the city may be summed up in a sentence often repeated, 'The spirit of the people is unbroken, but their nerve has gone'. That is to say, though they have been badly shaken by their experiences and are afraid, they do not want to give in. The ability to return to normal may be seen in the way cinemas begin to fill and shelters to empty as soon as there is a lull....

The following are danger points:– ...

(5) Lack of home or school discipline for children.

(6) Widespread looting.

(7) The lack of community spirit, shown in this looting of bombed persons and also in the fact that no attempt is made by the people to organise shelters or appoint marshals, and in the reluctance to take fire-watching duty. The paternalism of the authorities may foster this and it may be, in part, temperamental. The danger should be recognised as, in a crisis, panic may spread amongst a collection of people where there is no group feeling and everyone acts for himself.

'Special report on Portsmouth', Home Intelligence report, 19–24 May 1941, INF 1/292, Public Record Office, London.

7.4 Morale in Merseyside

In some cities the bombing raids appear to have increased resentment against minority groups.

The people seem fatalistic and there is unusual family solidarity, encouraged by the Catholic element. Though they are dour by temperament and have not the cockney resilience, they stood their eight-day ordeal with fortitude and seem able to readjust to normal conditions. As in Portsmouth, it was remarked that the morale of the 'near-bombed' suffered more than that of the bombed. It was also said that people were ready to help themselves until they realised there was official help available. They then expected everything done for them.

There seems some resentment against the authorities who are accused of trying to force people to stay in the city during bombing, by making it difficult for them to get out. Unless they can sleep where they feel safe, there is some fear that they might get out of control in a new crisis....

A symptom which may indicate fear is the distrust of foreign elements. Anti-Jewish feeling is said to be growing. Jews are supposed to be cowards who have fled to the best billets in safe areas and who avoid fire-watching duties. One restaurant recently refused to serve Jewish customers. Greeks are also disliked and there are occasional outbursts against the Chinese in shelters, though they give no trouble and are cleaner than the general shelter population.... In brief there seems to be a need to have someone to blame, and someone to act as scapegoat to work off the people's own fears.

The prevalence of rumours, such as the story that 30,000 were killed in the blitz, and that incendiary envelopes were to be dropped, is another sign of weakness.

'Special report on Merseyside', Home Intelligence report, July 1941, INF 1/292, Public Record Office, London.

7.5   London and the flying-bomb attacks, 1944

In some respects the morale of Londoners during the 1944 attacks by the V-1 and V-2 flying bombs seemed worse than during the Blitz. During the earlier raids by bombers Londoners usually had time to seek shelter, but this was often not possible during the flying-bomb attacks.

Evacuation has taken place on a considerable scale among those who could get away, particularly women with children, who are said to be crowding the main line stations all day. Urgent enquiries as to how to get out of London are reported from many W.V.S. [Women's Voluntary Services] and C.A.B. [Citizens' Advice Bureaux] centres.

There is reported to be a growing demand for an official evacuation scheme, particularly for children. People are angry, in the belief that no plan has been put into operation, and attempts to get away are, in a few instances, said to be 'verging on panic'....

Sheltering has become 'the next best thing to evacuation' for a great many Londoners. In some parts there is a general rush to the shelters when a bomb is heard, and men are said to show little signs of the 'women and children first' spirit.

Many more people are sleeping in shelters, both public and private, than was noticed in the blitz, and some are said to refuse to leave shelters day or night.

'London', Home Intelligence report, 6 July 1944, INF 1/292, Public Record Office, London.

8

Urban and rural

The Barlow, Scott and Uthwatt reports in the early years of the war created optimism that planning for land use would be one of the important wartime accomplishments. Instead, it proved to be an issue on which Labour and the Conservatives differed irreconcilably. The problem of land ownership was the 'real rock on which the Coalition [government] was broken'.[1]

8.1 Barlow Report

The Barlow Report was crucial to the wartime planning movement because it claimed that a central planning authority responsible for national planning was essential.

428. The [Royal] Commission unanimously accepted the following ... conclusions:

(1) In view of the nature and urgency of the problems ... national action is necessary.

(2) For this purpose, a Central Authority, national in scope and character is required.

(3) The activities of this Authority should be distinct from and should extend beyond those within the powers of any existing Government Department.

(4) The objectives of national action should be:

    (a) Continued and further redevelopment of congested urban areas, where necessary.

    (b) Decentralisation or dispersal, both of industries and industrial population, from such areas.

[1] Michael Foot, *Aneurin Bevan: A Biography, Vol. 1, 1897–1945*, London, 1962, p. 474.

(c) Encouragement of a reasonable balance of industrial development, so far as possible, throughout the various divisions or regions of Great Britain.

Report of the Royal Commission on the Distribution of the Industrial Population (Barlow Report), Cmd 6153, London, 1940, pp. 201–2.

8.2 Toward a green and pleasant land: the Scott Report

The Scott Report recommended planning to protect valuable agricultural land from being used for industrial or urban development. It also advocated improving access to the countryside by creating National Parks and by protecting footpaths through rural areas.

This summary is set out in the same order as the matters are considered in the body of the Report and no order of precedence is implied.

Access to the Countryside.

(i) There must be facility of access for all to the countryside but this must not interfere with the proper use of land in the national interest....

Footpaths and Bridle-paths....

(iv) The local authority should be under a statutory obligation to supervise and keep up footpaths....

National and Regional Parks and Other Open Spaces.

(i) National Parks should be delimited and a National Parks Authority set up....

Industry in Country Areas.

Extractive Industries.

(i) Extractive industries ... should be subject to effective planning control.

(ii) In principle it is wrong that any body or person should be allowed to work land for the extraction of minerals and leave it in a derelict condition. Legislation should be passed imposing an obligation on all those who derive benefit from the working of land for minerals to restore that land for agriculture or afforestation or other purposes within a short specified period of time after the land has been worked out....

Housing and Planning in Country Areas....

(iii) As far as possible tracts of good soil in the neighbourhood of towns and villages should be kept for the dual purpose of open spaces and market gardens and allotments and accordingly allotment holders should have security of tenure instead of the liability of being displaced by housing development....

(v) The area and delimitation of 'green belts' should be agreed with the Ministry of Agriculture.

(vi) Agricultural, soil, and land classification surveys should be made round each expanding urban area with the object of directing housing and other construction towards less productive land and of preventing the disruption of farm units.

(vii) New satellite towns, housing estates, garden cities and suburbs should be sited wherever practicable away from the better farm land and due attention should be paid to agricultural considerations in their siting....

Planning.

All land should be planned both nationally and locally.

Report of the Committee on Land Utilisation in Rural Areas (Scott Report), Cmd 6378, London, 1942, pp. 91, 93–4, 96–7.

8.3   Uthwatt Report

Land planning required a policy for compensation and betterment. Although it rejected land nationalisation, the Uthwatt Committee's proposals would have substantially increased the central government's powers.

49. We recommend the immediate vesting in the State of the rights of development in all land lying outside built-up areas (subject to certain exceptions) on payment of fair compensation, such vesting to be secured by the imposition of a prohibition against development otherwise than with the consent of the State accompanied by the grant of compulsory powers of acquiring the

land itself when wanted for public purposes or approved private development.

This measure of unification in the State of the development rights attaching to undeveloped land outside built-up areas is an essential minimum necessary to remove the conflict between public and private interest to which we have referred. As regards the area to which it applies, it is a complete solution of the hoary and vexing problem of shifting values. The development value for all time will have been acquired, and paid for. Compensation will no longer be a factor hindering the preparation and execution of proper planning schemes. The scheme will thus facilitate the operation of a positive policy for agriculture, the improvement of road systems and public services, the preservation of beauty spots and coastal areas, the reservation of green belts and National Parks, the control over the expansion of existing towns and cities, the establishment of satellite towns and the planned location of industry in new areas.

50. We recommend the conferment upon public authorities of powers of purchase, much wider and simpler in operation than under existing legislation.

If it is accepted, as we think it has to be, that fair compensation must be paid to an owner whose existing interest in land is required for planning purposes, it must be recognised that, in so far as the difficulties of the past arose merely from the necessity of paying this compensation, there is no remedy. Values have attached to land on the basis of the existing system of ownership and, short of confiscatory measures, it will always be costly to make land in private ownership available for planning purposes....

51. Inasmuch as sound planning does not destroy total land values but merely redistributes them, the ultimate cost may be reduced by recoupment elsewhere. The 'development rights scheme' will enable the State to secure the benefit of any shift of values to undeveloped land. Purchase of other land for recoupment ... will enable much of the shift within the area of towns to be collected for the public purse. The main defect in the structure of our scheme is that increased values may still accrue in part to land which for the time being remains to the full in private ownership.

We therefore recommend a scheme for the imposition of a periodic levy on increases in annual site value, with the object of securing such betterment for the community as and when it is realised, enjoyed, or realisable.

Report of the Committee on Compensation and Betterment (Uthwatt Report), Cmd 6386, London, 1942, pp. 27–9.

8.4 Conservatives and the Uthwatt Report

Alarmed by the popularity of planning, the Conservative Party sought to deflect support from the Uthwatt Report by offering an alternative.

In these days when every street corner orator is talking of a 'Planned Economy' or 'Planning for Plenty' we think it is essential that the Conservative Party should not give the impression that it is not interested, when public opinion appears to demand some further development of planning. Further, when the Archbishop of Canterbury has already said that we must not allow the Uthwatt proposals to be whittled away by vested interests, it is most important that the Conservative Party should clarify which of the Uthwatt objectives it shares and emphasise that it is not meeting either aspirations or suggested methods of approach by blank negation.

... it is relevant to consider the feeling in the Party with regard to this proposal as far as it has disclosed itself. It must be remembered that the technical difficulty of the report has delayed the formation and publication of opinion and therefore that silence does not mean acquiescence.

We understand that opinions in the Central Landowners' Association, the Land Agents' Society, are definitely against the Development Rights Scheme. We think, on the other hand, there is a definite feeling among the public that something must be done to insure that excessive compensation is not paid and that betterment is secured to the public. Many of the urban section of the Party would therefore view the proposal with indifference if not active support.

In these circumstances we feel that it is most important that the attitude of the Party should not be merely negative.... The counterproposal that was put before us was –

Any large landowner developing part of his estate gives up a certain proportion of land for open spaces, squares, roads, playing fields, etc., he gets no payment for this land but he has the value in the sites on the rest of the land. The suggestion is that this surrender of land should be compulsory for every developer. Be his area large or small he should surrender some fixed proportion, say 20% free, for public purposes....

We are not prepared to give final judgment as to whether the alternative fully solves the problem propounded by the Uthwatt Committee. We feel however, that the existence of the alternative (which would require careful elaboration and analysis of the suggested details) justified the attitude that a decision on the development rights scheme should be postponed.

Sir David Maxwell Fyfe (Committee Chairman) to James Stuart (Conservative Party whip), 'Report of the Conservative [Party] Committee on the Uthwatt report', 5 May 1942, HLG 81/38, Public Record Office, London.

8.5   Conflict over Uthwatt

Whatever consensus may have existed on other issues, it did not extend to the Uthwatt proposals. They became the focus of intense party conflict.

The main proposal of the Uthwatt Committee for undeveloped land outside built-up areas is that there should be an 'immediate vesting in the State of the rights of development in all land lying outside built-up areas (subject to certain exceptions) on payment of fair compensation...'.

On taking office the Minister [of Town and Country Planning] immediately proceeded to make an exhaustive examination of the problem. By this time many alternative suggestions had been tabled and all of these were subjected to critical analysis. Most of them, although not all, accepted the idea of a universal control over undeveloped land, but views as to fair compensation were widely divergent; and several schemes advocated a postponement, in whole or part, of compensation, thus entailing a radical departure from one of Uthwatt's essentials. A further complication arose from the growing criticism directed against Uthwatt's tripartite separation of undeveloped land outside built-up areas, undeveloped land inside built-up areas, and developed land.

The Minister was in sympathy with this last-named criticism, and in an alternative scheme which he has propounded, one and the same form of solution is applied to all classes of land having a development or redevelopment value for new use. The outstanding feature of this scheme is that the universal control only carries with it re-imbursement for actual out-of-pocket loss....

Of recent weeks the Minister has been exploring the matter informally with some of his Conservative colleagues, and has met with the same sharp division of opinion mainly on the financial issue. Where opposition exists, it is directed against both the Uthwatt method of 'global' assessment and against the Minister's own alternative of 'out-of-pocket loss'.

The question comes down to this – what is politically practicable?

'Uthwatt report', S. Phillips to J. H. Peck (member of the Prime Minister's private secretariat), September 1943, PREM 4/92/2, Public Record Office, London.

8.6   The compensation problem

Although it was committed to planning and accepted that control of land was necessary for planning to be implemented, the government was unable to agree on the problem of compensation.

After a recent conversation with Mr. W. S. Morrison's private secretary, I understand that the situation reduced to its simplest terms is roughly the following:–

1. H.M.G. [His Majesty's Government] are publicly committed to the establishment of a planning authority and to the principle of control of land utilisation by the Central and Local authorities....

3. The principal stumbling block in all schemes for establishing control over the use of land is a financial one which has far-reaching political implications, namely, the question of compensation. The administrative aspect of control involves no serious difficulties and if there were unlimited funds available its introduction would be a simple matter. As it is the Government's

commitments can only be carried out if a satisfactory plan for compensation and betterment can be evolved and accepted by Parliament.

4. The proposals of the Uthwatt Committee have been thoroughly examined and rejected. An alternative scheme has been proposed by the Minister of Town and Country Planning. The scheme, while it is claimed to be administratively practicable and profitable, is likely to meet with very strong political opposition on the grounds that it is unfair to land and property owners.

'Town and country planning', memorandum by J. H. Peck to Mr Martin (Churchill's principal Private Secretary), 15 September 1943, PREM 4/92/2, Public Record Office, London.

8.7 Town and Country Planning Bill

Unable to reach agreement on the fundamental issues of compensation and betterment, the Cabinet was forced to delay introducing its Town and Country Planning Bill.

The following points arose in discussion:–

(a) The view was expressed that it would be undesirable to publish the Bill until the Government were ready to publish the White Paper on Compensation and Betterment. Agreement had not yet been reached among Ministers on the problems dealt with in the White Paper, and there was no guarantee that its terms would have been agreed in time to allow of its being published with the Bill if the Bill was introduced before Whitsun....

(d) It was pointed out that the Uthwatt Committee had recommended March 1939 value as a ceiling for the price to be paid for land acquired for public purposes. The Bill, however, provided for the adoption of March 1939 value as the standard in all cases of compulsory acquisition. The result was that local authorities would probably have to pay the March 1939 value in all cases, whereas at present they could sometimes buy at a lower figure. There was likely to be considerable criticism of this in the House of Commons....

The general feeling of the War Cabinet was that, despite the criticism to which the Government were being subjected for delay in introducing the Bill, it would be better to defer its introduction for a short time.

War Cabinet minute, 24 May 1944, CAB 65/42, WM (44) 68, Public Record Office, London.

8.8   Controlling land use

Irreconcilably divided, the Reconstruction Committee[2] finally proposed to put a scheme before Parliament which was not the government's final position in order to encourage public debate of the issues.

During the past six months the Reconstruction Committee have devoted a large proportion of their time to the search for an effective means of controlling the use of land in order to provide a solid foundation for the physical reconstruction of our towns and countryside after the war.

2. Proposals based on the recommendations of the Uthwatt Report for the development rights and an annual levy on site values would be hotly contested in Parliament; and the Committee have, therefore, sought an alternative solution which might command a more general measure of support.

After long deliberation they have reached agreement on the scheme outlined in the attached draft of a White Paper. This is admittedly a compromise between the widely differing views which are held on this subject by different members of the Committee. But those views reflect a similar divergence of opinion in Parliament and in the country; and no scheme which was not a compromise would be likely to prove generally acceptable.

3. The Reconstruction Committee are unanimous in commending this scheme to the War Cabinet for early presentation to Parliament – not as representing the Government's final views, but, as is made clear in the Foreword to the White Paper, in order to focus public discussion of the issues involved, and to assure themselves that there would be a substantial measure of public support for a solution on these lines.

'Town and country planning: the control of land use', memorandum by the Minister of Reconstruction, 10 June 1944, CAB 66/51, WP (44) 311, Public Record Office, London.

---

[2] A War Cabinet committee created in 1943 when the Ministry of Reconstruction was established.

8.9 Town and Country Planning Bill revisited

After the War Cabinet sent the Town and Country Planning Bill back to the Reconstruction Committee, the differences between Labour and Conservatives remained so profound that at least one Conservative, Lord Selborne, threatened to resign because he considered the Bill a threat to property rights.

2. The two matters which the War Cabinet had particularly in mind in deciding to postpone further consideration of the Bill (namely (a) the question of the 1939 standard and (b) the question whether the procedure proposed by the Bill for the acquisition of land for the redevelopment of war-damaged and obsolescent areas is sufficiently expeditious) have been reconsidered by the Reconstruction Committee.

The 1939 Standard.

3. The Reconstruction Committee unanimously reaffirmed their decision that the provisions of the Bill under which the price payable for public acquisition of land would in general be based on 1939 prices but could, in the case of certain owner-occupiers, be increased so as to take account of the cost of reinstatement, should stand as drafted. The Minister of Economic Warfare [Viscount Selborne] who had an opportunity of supporting his memorandum at the meeting of the Committee asked that this dissent from the conclusion should be recorded.

Procedure for Acquisition.

4. On review of this matter the Reconstruction Committee agreed that the procedure for compulsory acquisition of land prescribed by the Bill could be justified to Parliament as sufficient to meet essential needs.

The Committee were, however, of the opinion that the provisions of the Bill as drafted were open to the objection that owners might be under an indeterminate threat of compulsory acquisition which would inflict hardship on them. The Bill has now been amended with a view to meeting this objection.

'Town and Country Planning Bill', memorandum by W. S. Morrison (Minister of Town and Country Planning), 13 June 1944, CAB 66/51, WP (44) 310, Public Record Office, London.

8.10   White paper on land use

Unable to resolve their differences over land use, the
Cabinet decided to issue a white paper as the basis for
discussion. Portraying the white paper as an example of
consensus is misleading because it did not represent an
agreed policy and it was eventually shelved without being
voted on by Parliament.

1. Provision for the right use of land, in accordance with a
considered policy, is an essential requirement of the Government's
programme of post-war reconstruction. New houses, whether of
permanent or emergency construction; the new lay-out of areas
devastated by enemy action or blighted by reason of age or bad
living conditions; ... the preservation of land for national parks
and forests, ... – all these related parts of a single reconstruction
programme involve the use of land, and it is essential that their
various claims on land should be so harmonised as to ensure for
the people of this country the greatest possible measure of
individual well-being and national prosperity....

But there will still remain to be corrected what is generally
agreed to be the defect which most of all prevented or distorted
good planning before the war – namely the state of the law
regarding the payment of compensation to landowners affected
by planning schemes, and the collection of 'betterment' from
those who benefit therefrom....

6. The present Paper is therefore mainly devoted to the consideration of this problem of compensation and betterment....

13. The Government accept as substantially correct the Uthwatt
Committee's analysis of the problems with which their Report
deals. There would, however, be serious practical difficulties in
adopting as a whole the particular proposals suggested by the
Committee for solving those problems. These difficulties may be
summarised as follows:–

    (a) The recommendations provide substantially different
       treatment for
       (i)   owners of undeveloped land outside town areas;
       (ii) owners of undeveloped land inside town areas;
       (iii) owners of developed land....

14. The Government accept in principle the recommendations
of the Uthwatt Committee regarding the public acquisition of

land in areas requiring redevelopment as a whole, and provisions for this purpose are included in the Bill now before Parliament. For the reasons outlined in paragraph 13 above, however, they find themselves unable to adopt the Committee's detailed proposals for dealing with the problems of compensation and betterment. After the most careful consideration the Government put forward the following general scheme as to that which, in their view, detailed proposals should conform. They present this description of the scheme in order that Parliament and the public may have an opportunity for full discussion of these far-reaching measures before detailed proposals for further legislation are formulated; and they will take their final decisions in the light of those discussions....

16. The general scheme put forward by the Government would include the following main provisions:–

Powers of Public Acquisition.

(a) The power of public purchase of land will be made available to Local Authorities, with the consent of the Minister concerned:–

(b) The purchase price to be paid on public acquisition of land will, for a period of five years, be fixed on the standard of value ruling on 31st march, 1939....

Betterment Charge.

(e) Owners of land, whether developed or undeveloped, will for the future, whenever permission is granted to develop or redevelop for a different use, be subject to a Betterment Charge at the rate of 80 per cent of the increase in the value of the land due to the granting of permission – i.e. 80 per cent of the difference between the value of the land with the benefit of the permission and its value if permission had been refused. In those cases where refusal would have attracted compensation, a suitable set-off for such compensation should be made from the Betterment Charge.

Compensation.

(f) Owners of land, whether developed or undeveloped, which on 31st March, 1939, had some developmental value will upon any future refusal of permission to develop or redevelop, be entitled (except where under the present law either no compensation or only restricted compensation would have been payable) to be paid fair compensation in respect of the loss of development value existing on 31st March, 1939, but will not be entitled to any compensation in respect of any further development value accruing after the 31st March 1939....

21. This proposal involves two important departures from the recommendation of the Uthwatt Committee. First, the Committee's recommendation was limited to undeveloped land outside town areas. The Government's proposal extends to all land, wherever it may be, and whether built-on or unbuilt on. Secondly, the Uthwatt Committee recommended that where consent for development has been given, the State should itself purchase the land and lease it to the applicant. Although purchase will be necessary in some cases, the Government's proposal is that the control should be operated in the main through the granting of consents or licences to develop.

'The control of land use', *Parliamentary Papers, 1943–44*, vol. 8, Cmd 6537, London, 1944, pp. 3–4, 6–10.

8.11   Public opinion

Although public support for the Uthwatt Report never approached the level given to the Beveridge Report, there was concern that rejecting the Uthwatt proposals would adversely affect efforts to rebuild Britain when the war ended.

(d) *Town and country planning* (Ten regions): Some interest is reported, particularly in bombed towns; people want to know about rebuilding plans and what assistance the Government proposes to give.

The Government proposals for the control of land, and the rejection of the Uthwatt proposals for balancing compensation and betterment ... continue to cause dissatisfaction and disappointment. It is felt that landowners are 'winning the day', that speculation will not now be eliminated, and that the price of houses and the speed with which they are erected will be adversely affected. Local authorities are said to feel they will not now get sufficient backing, and to be critical of the proposed plans for requisitioning land.

'Town and country planning', Home Intelligence report, 20 July 1944, INF 1/292, Public Record Office, London.

8.12 Opposition to planning legislation

> The government's Town and Country Planning Bill aroused intense hostility from landowners and back-bench Conserv-atives and drew attention to the fundamental differences between Labour and the Conservatives on land policy.

6. Clauses 45 and 46 (dealing with compensation) are of great importance. To the clauses as they stand, the C.L.A. [Central Landowners' Association] takes strong exception.... In the view of the C.L.A. the following changes in Clause 45 are necessary:
  (1) All improvements carried out since 1939 should be paid for at their actual cost, less fair wear and tear....
  (2) An all-round addition should be made to 1939 prices to allow for the decreased value of money.
  In other words, for '1939 price' there would be substituted '1939 value', as the writers of the Uthwatt Report contemplated.
  (3) There should be an over-riding provision that no land should be compulsorily acquired at less than its post-war agri-cultural value.

'Observations on the Town and Country Planning Bill, 1944', memor-andum by the Central Landowners' Association, August 1944, CAB 124/375, Public Record Office, London.

8.13 Housing

> In the final year of the war, housing became one of the issues about which the public was most concerned. The delay in developing a plan for house building was linked to the perception that the government's attempt to develop a land-use policy had failed.

Housing and employment continue to cause most talk and most anxiety.

The main differences this month are a considerable increase in comment about (a) the need of a land policy as a preliminary to solving the housing problem; (b) local authorities being unable to proceed with housing plans....

Housing (All Regions): Gloom and despair are widespread, and people now think it will be years before everyone is adequately housed; they fear the present 'hopeless' position will only be accentuated when demobilization starts. The Government is widely criticised for making 'no real effort'; plans so far announced are thought totally inadequate – 'it must be done in a big way'. People are very anxious indeed that there should be homes for the Forces to come back to; the men themselves are said to expect housing to be provided. Many people think a building programme should be started immediately.

A number of people (Five Regions) blame the delay on the Government's 'failure' to evolve a policy for the acquisition of land; too much deference to land and property owners is suspected, and people resent houses for servicemen 'being delayed for this'. Nationalization, or at least strict Government control, is urged 'if things are ever going to be done properly'. Local authorities are said to have their hands tied (Five Regions) – unable to make a start even with the preparation of sites.

'Post-war reconstruction', Home Intelligence report, 12 October 1944, INF 1/292, Public Record Office, London.

9

Social insurance

The 1942 Beveridge report proposed a universal scheme of social security against poverty. Although public support for the plan was unexpectedly strong, reservations were expressed by powerful groups while it was being drafted, and by a secret Conservative Party committee after it was published. Public pressure forced a reluctant government to endorse the report, but critics were successful in modifying Beveridge's proposals in the white paper.

9.1 Employers and reform

Although it endorsed a national compulsory contributory insurance system, the British Employers' Confederation warned against a more expensive scheme of the type Beveridge was contemplating.

In the building up of our State insurance systems for Unemployment, Health and Pensions, the Confederation has supported the principle of a national compulsory contributory system as an integral part of our industrial life....

The Confederation has throughout, however, maintained that it is imperative that the expenditure on these Services, and the other Social Services, must be directly related to the industrial performance of the country on which they ultimately depend for their continuance, and that the benefits they provide should not be such as to weaken the incentive of the population to play their full part in maintaining the productivity and exporting ability of the country at its highest level....

In the light of these considerations, the Confederation regards it as essential in the first place that any proposals for a new or revised Social Services system to operate after the present war

116

should be framed with due regard to the potential post-war economic position of the country....

Indeed, it seems to the Confederation, in the light of these imponderable factors, that nothing would be more dangerous from the standpoint of post-war reconstruction than to hold out assurances which subsequent events may make impossible of fulfilment.

'Post-war reconstruction – social services', memorandum from the British Employers' Confederation to the Beveridge Committee, 13 May 1942, CAB 87/79, SIC (42) 49, Public Record Office, London.

9.2 Opposition to reform

> While Beveridge's proposals had wide public support, some groups, including the British Employers' Confederation, did not share that enthusiasm, but did not wish to make their reservations public.

A ... [Sir John Forbes Watson, Director, British Employers' Confederation] On the question of what we say now, a good deal of what we say may depend upon whether it is private and confidential....

2818 Q. No, no, not publish it without reference to you. – A. [Watson] Therefore, before you issue your report you would submit to us anything we may say today that you may wish to quote.

2819 Q. Yes. – A. [Watson] That would make a difference to us because, naturally, in writing an official statement of this sort we have had to observe certain considerations. There are deeper thoughts which possibly this afternoon we might express....

I want to say here – it will be on the shorthand note, but I do not know that I want to say it publicly – we did not start this war with Germany in order to improve our social services; the war was forced upon us by Germany and we entered it to preserve our freedom and to keep the Gestapo outside our houses, and that is what the war means. Having entered it, we are now told we must have better conditions in order to win it, but I personally refuse to believe it....

In the letter he wrote to you Sir William Jowitt said:– 'It must be regarded as to some extent a war measure in giving to the public assurance that plans are being made for greatly improved social conditions after the war'. I do not think we share that view.

British Employers' Confederation testimony to the Beveridge Committee, eleventh meeting, 20 May 1942, CAB 87/77, SIC (42), Public Record Office, London.

9.3   The Beveridge Report

The Beveridge Report proposed establishing a social security system that would protect all citizens against poverty by providing a guaranteed subsistence income.

9. The third principle is that social security must be achieved by co-operation between the State and the individual. The State should offer security for service and contribution. The State in organising security should not stifle incentive, opportunity, responsibility: in establishing a national minimum, it should leave room and encouragement for voluntary action by each individual to provide more than that minimum for himself and his family....

21. The first view is that benefit in return for contributions, rather than free allowances from the State, is what the people of Britain desire.... [This desire] is shown in another way by the strength of popular objection to any kind of means test. This objection springs not so much from a desire to get everything for nothing, as from resentment at a provision which appears to penalise what people have come to regard as the duty and pleasure of thrift....

22. The second view is that whatever money is required for provision of insurance benefits ... should come from a Fund to which the recipients have contributed and to which they may be required to make larger contributions if the Fund proves inadequate. The plan adopted since 1930 in regard to prolonged unemployment ... that the State should take this burden off insurance, in order to keep the contribution down, is wrong in principle. The insured persons should not feel that income for idleness, however caused, can come from a bottomless purse....

233. The problem of the nature and extent of the provision to be made for old age is the most important, and in some ways the most difficult, of all the problems of social security....

It is dangerous to be in any way lavish to old age, until adequate provision has been assured for all other vital needs, such as the prevention of disease and the adequate nutrition of the young....

239. Any Plan of Social Security worthy of its name must ensure that every citizen, fulfilling during his working life the obligation of service according to his powers, can claim as of right when he is past work an income adequate to maintain him. This means providing, as an essential part of the plan, a pension on retirement from work which is enough for subsistence.... It means also providing a pension which is not reduced if the pensioner has resources. On the contrary, direct encouragement of voluntary insurance or saving to meet abnormal needs or to maintain standards of comfort above subsistence level, is an essential part of the Plan for Social Security proposed in this Report....

240. ... it is important that the coming into operation of a scheme of adequate pensions given as of right should be gradual....

The pensions proposed in the Plan for Social Security are retirement pensions, not old age pensions. There is no fixed age for retirement, but only a minimum pension age, 65 for men and 60 for women, at or after which each individual has the option of retiring and claiming pension....

245. Making receipt of pension conditional on retirement is not intended to encourage or hasten retirement. On the contrary, the conditions governing pension should be such as to encourage every person who can to go on working after reaching pensionable age, and to postpone retirement and the claiming of pension. The large and growing proportion of the total population who will be above the pensionable ages of 65 for men and 60 for women, makes it essential to raise the average age of retirement....

300. *Scope of Social Security*: The term 'social security' is used here to denote the securing of an income to take the place of earnings when they are interrupted by unemployment, sickness or accident, to provide for retirement through age, to provide

against loss of support by the death of another person and to meet exceptional expenditures, such as those connected with birth, death, and marriage. Primarily social security means security of income up to a minimum, but the provision of an income should be associated with treatment designed to bring the interruption of earnings to an end as soon as possible.

301. *Three Assumptions*: No satisfactory scheme of social security can be devised except on the following assumptions:–

(A) Children's allowances for children up to the age of 15 or if in full-time education up to the age of 16;

(B) Comprehensive health and rehabilitation services for prevention and cure of disease and restoration of capacity for work, available to all members of the community;

(C) Maintenance of employment, that is to say avoidance of mass unemployment....

304. *Flat Rate of Subsistence Benefit*: The first fundamental principle of the social insurance scheme is provision of a flat rate of insurance benefit, irrespective of the amount of the earnings which have been interrupted by unemployment or disability or ended by retirement....

305. *Flat Rate of Contribution*: The second fundamental principle of the scheme is that the compulsory contribution required of each insured person or his employer is at a flat rate, irrespective of his means. All insured persons, rich or poor, will pay the same contributions for the same security....

306. *Unification of Administrative Responsibility*: The third fundamental principle is unification of administrative responsibility in the interests of efficiency and economy. For each insured person there will be a single weekly contribution, in respect of all his benefits....

307. *Adequacy of Benefit*: The fourth fundamental principle is adequacy of benefit in amount and in time. The flat rate of benefit proposed is intended in itself to be sufficient without further resources to provide the minimum income needed for subsistence in all normal cases.... The benefits are adequate also in time, that is to say except for contingencies of a temporary nature, they will continue indefinitely without means test, so long as the need continues, though subject to any change of conditions

and treatment required by prolongation of the interruption in earning and occupation.

308. *Comprehensiveness*: The fifth fundamental principle is that social insurance should be comprehensive, in respect both of the persons covered and of their needs. It should not leave either to national assistance or to voluntary insurance any risk so general or so uniform that social insurance can be justified. For national assistance involves a means test which may discourage voluntary insurance or personal saving....

339. *Marriage needs*: For the purpose of the Social Insurance scheme housewives form a special Class (III). Every woman on marriage will become a new person, acquiring new rights and not carrying on into marriage claims to unemployment or disability benefit in respect of contribution made before marriage. Some new rights, as for marriage grant and maternity grant, apply to all married women; all women also during marriage will continue to acquire qualifications for pensions in old age through contributions made by their husbands. Some of the new rights, as for share of benefit due to husband's unemployment or disability, apply only to married women who are not gainfully occupied. Some, as for maternity benefit in addition to maternity grant, apply only to married women who are gainfully occupied....

347. *End of Marriage otherwise than by Widowhood*: Divorce, legal separation, desertion and voluntary separation may cause needs similar to those caused by widowhood.... But from the point of view of the woman, loss of her maintenance as a housewife without her consent and not through her fault, is one of the risks of marriage against which she should be insured; she should not depend on assistance. Recognition of housewives as a distinct insurance class, performing necessary service not for pay, implies that, if the marriage ends otherwise than by widowhood, she is entitled to the same provision as for widowhood, unless the marriage maintenance has ended through her fault or voluntary action without just cause. That is to say, subject to the practical considerations mentioned in the note below she should get temporary separation benefit (on the same lines as widow's benefit), and guardian or training benefit where appropriate.

NOTE. – The principle that a married woman who without fault loses the maintenance to which she is entitled from her husband should get benefit is clear. It is obvious, however, that except where the maintenance has ended through divorce or other form of legal separation establishing that the fault is not that of the wife, considerable practical difficulties may arise in determining whether a claim of benefit, as distinct from assistance, has arisen. There will often be difficulty in determining responsibility for the break-up of the marriage....

348. *Unmarried Person Living as a Wife*: Treatment of this problem, complicated by the possibility that either or both parties in this extra-legal relation may have a legal spouse, is necessarily difficult....

(iii) Maternity grant and maternity benefit raise the most difficult of all questions in this connection. On the one hand, it may be said that, in the interests of the child, grant and benefit should be paid where appropriate, irrespective of the marital relation of the parents. Against this it may be said that the interest of the State is not in getting children born, but in getting them born in conditions which secure to them the proper domestic environment and care. The decision in regard to maternity grant may depend on whether or not it is thought to be practicable and desirable administratively to require previous registration of an adult dependant. In that case a man who has an unmarried person living with him as his wife, on registering this, would be qualified to obtain dependant allowance for her during unemployment and disability and maternity grant also. In regard to maternity benefit, in spite of the fact that this is for married women to some extent a compensation for lower unemployment and disability benefits if gainfully occupied, it will probably be felt right, in the interests of the child, to make this benefit equally available to unmarried mothers, so that they may have the same opportunity of withdrawing from gainful occupation at the time of the confinement....

373. ... At the basis of any system of social security covering all those who comply with reasonable just conditions for

insurance and assistance, there must be provision for a limited class of men or women who through weakness or badness of character fail to comply. In the last resort the man who fails to comply with the conditions for obtaining benefit or assistance and leaves his family without resources must be subject to penal treatment....

440. There are five reasons for saying that a satisfactory scheme of social insurance assumes the maintenance of employment and the prevention of mass unemployment....

First, payment of unconditional cash benefits as of right during unemployment is satisfactory provision only for short periods of unemployment; after that, complete idleness even on income demoralises. The proposal of the Report accordingly is to make unemployment benefit after a certain period conditional upon attendance at a work or training centre. But this proposal is impracticable, if it has to be applied to men by the million....

Fifth, though it should be within the power of the community to bear the cost of the whole Plan for Social Security, the cost is heavy and, if to the necessary cost waste is added, it may become insupportable. Unemployment, both through increasing expenditure on benefit and through reducing the income to bear on those costs, is the worst form of waste....

449. ... Abolition of want cannot be brought about merely by increasing production, without seeing to correct distribution of the product; but correct distribution does not mean what it has often been taken to mean in the past – distribution between the different agents in production, between land, capital, management and labour. Better distribution of purchasing power is required among wage-earners themselves, as between times of earning and not earning, and between times of heavy family responsibilities and of light or no family responsibilities.

Social Insurance and Allied Services (Beveridge Report), Cmd 6404, London, 1942, pp. 6, 11–12, 90, 92, 93, 96, 120, 122, 131, 134–5, 154.

9.4 Conservative reaction to the Report

Although reluctant for political reasons to oppose it openly, Conservative MPs did not welcome Beveridge's scheme and would have preferred postponing considering it until after the war.

The Lobbies are buzzing with comment on the Beveridge Report. The 1922 Committee were addressed by Beveridge and gave him a cordial reception. The Tory line seems to be to welcome the Report in principle, and then to whittle it away by detailed criticism. They will say that it is all very splendid and Utopian, but we can only begin to know whether we can afford it once we have some idea what our foreign trade will be like after the war. They also suggest that in many ways it is an incentive to idleness, that some people are better off under the present arrangements, and that in fact it is the old Poor Law immensely magnified.

Harold Nicolson, diary entry for 2 December 1942, in Nigel Nicolson (ed.), *Harold Nicolson. Diaries and Letters 1939–1945*, London, 1967, p. 264.

9.5   Can the nation afford it?

> Ralph Assheton, who became the Conservative Party Chairman in 1944, directed the attention of the secret Conservative Party committee reviewing the Beveridge Report to the question of whether the nation could afford it in addition to other desirable objectives.

It is our aim as Conservatives to build up a brave, healthy and industrious population devoted to the cause of freedom and alive to the responsibilities which such a cause demands.

To achieve this aim we must first secure the safety of the realm and our own Empire from attack: this can only be done by maintaining strong armed forces and conducting ourselves so as to earn the respect and support of other nations.

Secondly we must honour financial obligations to those who have sacrificed their lives and limbs on our behalf and pay our debts.

Thirdly we must do what we can to maintain a reasonable level of social services....

Sir William Beveridge tells us that the life Giants we have to conquer are Want, Disease, Ignorance, Squalor, and Idleness. He claims that his plan – which is a very expensive one – will abolish one of these giants, i.e. Want, and it must be remembered that the cost of his plan does not cover any additional claims on the taxpayer for Housing and Education. It has always been and still is a principal aim of the Conservative Party to avoid poverty. Will this plan do so? Is it the best plan for the purpose? If so, can we afford it and should it take precedence over other claims?

These are the questions to which we must address ourselves.

Ralph Assheton, 'Beveridge Report Committee: note by the Chairman', 17 December 1942, Conservative Party Archive, CRD 2/28/6, Bodleian Library, Oxford.

9.6   Secret Conservative Party committee

Churchill had appointed this secret Conservative Party committee to review the Beveridge Report, and it claimed to represent the views of 90 per cent of Conservative back-bench MPs. It objected to several of the Report's key proposals, including the principles of universality and adequacy.

2. Sir William Beveridge's Report expresses the views of one man on a number of highly technical subjects, and although he had the advantage of the assistance of many eminent Civil Servants, the Report is his alone and does not contain, as is widely assumed, the recommendations of a well qualified expert Committee. There is no doubt, however, that the great publicity which the Report has received in the Press, on the platform and over the wireless has unfortunately led many people to assume that it represents Government policy and is likely to be carried into speedy effect as soon as the war is over....

4. Sir William Beveridge bases his recommendations on three assumptions:

Assumption (A)   Children's Allowances;
Assumption (B)   Comprehensive Health and Rehabilitation Services;
Assumption (C)   the Maintenance of Employment;

5. Without doubt Assumption (C) is the most vital, and is uppermost in the minds of the people. Unless we are able to

maintain a reasonable level of employment it is impossible to contemplate great additions to our expenditure. The whole scheme is one for sharing prosperity and if there is no sufficient prosperity to share it fails. It is clearly impossible accurately to forecast the employment situation after the war as we are as yet unaware, for example, what, if any, international agreements may be come to with regard to trade and currency....

7. The Committee by a majority is in favour of a scheme of children's allowances, subject to further consideration of the financial problem, and for many reasons we are inclined to favour allowances for all children, including the first, but at a lower level than that proposed by Sir William Beveridge.

One of the chief reasons in favour of including the first child is that if allowances for all children are paid, whether or not the parent is in employment, the temptation to evade work would be much less, since the financial advantage of doing so will not be increased by obtaining children's allowances as part of the Unemployment Benefit.... As to the rate of the children's allowance, the Committee felt that it should not be a subsistence allowance (except in clear cases for orphans) but it should be made clear that parental responsibility is not removed and that the allowances are made by the State for the purpose of making the bringing up of families easier and for dealing with want in large families....

8. With regard to Assumption (B), we accept the proposal that there should be a comprehensive health and rehabilitation service available to all citizens.... The majority of the Committee feel that all members of the community should be able to join such a scheme but that contributions to it should only be obligatory on those with incomes below a certain level. Some members of the Committee, however, hold the view that all citizens should be compelled to contribute.

It was agreed that on no account should steps be taken which would involve the complete obliteration of private practice or of independent voluntary hospitals, and if the preservation of private practice – which the Committee considers essential in the interests of medical science as well as desirable in itself – can only be maintained by leaving those above a certain income level outside the scope of the scheme, the Committee would accept that position.

9. We do not care for the phrase 'social security,' as experience has shown us that safety first is not the basis on which to form the policy of a great nation, nor is it even a successful political slogan. We should prefer, therefore, to talk of 'social insurance' rather than 'social security'....

13. Fourthly, ... the plan is one involving limited contributions by employers and workers and a contract of unlimited liability for the State. Is the State justified in assuming a liability of this kind to meet not only want but also to assure benefits to those not in need?

Much of this objection would disappear and the principle of insurance be more clearly established if the liability of the state was to add a fixed proportion of the contributions coming from others. Benefits in excess of those which would be so available would have to come through the medium of Assistance with a personal needs test.

14. We believe that at any rate unemployment insurance should continue to be dealt with by a separate Fund and that benefits must be related to the state of the Fund. Long-term unemployment is certainly not an insurable risk and it is not appropriate to deal with it as if it was. It is essential to preserve the incentive to work and it is necessary, therefore, that benefit should as a rule be substantially lower than wages.

We do not think that those who have been unemployed for more than six months should be entitled of right to unemployment benefit; we urge that this should be dependent upon their placing their services at the disposal of the State, which will be entitled to direct those seeking its aid either to be trained for work other than their own or to go to whatever work may be available for them at fair wages, whether in their own trade or not.

Appendix

8. Benefits

The Committee wish to emphasise that, because a number of people will receive weekly payments under a variety of benefits, whether in fact their own lack of resources make this socially necessary or not, the social insurance scheme goes further than the mere removal of want. So long as a scheme confines itself to the abolition of want, it is legitimate and necessary to vary the contributions and benefits in accordance with marked fluctuations in the cost of living. But as the scheme goes further than the abolition of want, the Committee view with considerable apprehension the proposed relationship of the level of contributions and benefit to the cost of living.

Conservative Party Committee, 'Report on the Beveridge proposals', 19 January 1943, Conservative Party Archive, CRD 2/28/6, Bodleian Library, Oxford.

9.7   Cabinet discussion of the Report

During the Cabinet discussion of the Beveridge Report, Conservative ministers opposed some of the scheme's central principles and sought to avoid any commitment to it.

The Chancellor of the Exchequer [Kingsley Wood] said that the question whether we could afford the expenditure involved in giving effect to the Beveridge Report was sure to be raised in the [House of Commons] Debate. From this point of view he attached the greatest importance to paragraphs 3–6 of the [Reconstruction Priorities] Committee's Report.[1] These paragraphs recommended that the Government spokesmen should make it clear that no firm commitments would be entered into at the present time, and that any statement of the Government's views of particular proposals in the Beveridge Plan were all subject to this general proviso.... These views were accepted.

The Paymaster-General [Lord Cherwell] thought it would be desirable to emphasise, even more strongly than in paragraph

---

[1] The War Cabinet Committee on Reconstruction Priorities was established in January 1943 to decide what position the government should take on the Beveridge Report in light of the split within the Cabinet between Conservative and Labour ministers. Although recommending that the government accept in principle Beveridge's proposals for children's allowances, a comprehensive health service, and the 'Maintenance of Employment', the committee concluded that postwar defence expenditure and industrial reconstruction should take priority over new social programmes, and therefore the government should avoid any firm commitment to the reforms Beveridge proposed until the cost of the former had been determined. 'The Beveridge Plan. Interim Report of the Committee on Reconstruction Priorities', 11 February 1943, CAB 66/34, Public Record Office, London.

four of the Committee's Report, the extent of the competing claims on the Exchequer, and to make it clear that, if Parliament wished the principles in the Beveridge Report to be accepted, this must mean that there would be less money available for other objects....

The Lord President of the Council [Sir John Anderson] said that there might be a strong feeling in the House that the State Insurance scheme should not be extended to classes which were not in need of State assistance. He thought that the War Cabinet ought to consider this point carefully.

The general view of the War Cabinet was in favour of making the plan of universal application....

Discussion ensued as to the principle in the Beveridge Report that the rates of benefit should be sufficient to provide, without further resources, the income required for subsistence in all normal cases. The view generally taken was that the subsistence principle involved review of the rates in the event of a material change in the cost of living, and that the embodiment of the principle in the scheme was therefore inconsistent with the fact that the scheme was contributory, the rates of contribution being closely related to the amount of benefit.

War Cabinet minute, 12 February 1943, CAB 65/33, WM 28 (43), Public Record Office, London.

9.8   Public reaction to the government's position

The government's initial unwillingness to endorse the Beveridge Report drew widespread criticism.

A. The majority, chiefly working-class people, who deplore the 'shelving of the Plan', and whose feelings are reported to vary from 'anger' to 'despondency' at the 'betrayal of their interests'. They blame:

   (i)   Vested interests for 'over-aweing the Government'. The opposition to the Catering Bill and to the Report are alleged to 'show the strength of the reactionary forces who want to go back to 1939', and it is suggested that 'they will have to be overcome before the Report will see fruition'.

(ii) The Government for 'their attitude to the Report', which is said to have created a good deal of 'pessimism and cynicism about the post-war world'. 'Why get Beveridge to make a plan at all, if you are going to turn it down?'

'The government and the Beveridge report', Home Intelligence report, 11 March 1943, INF 1/292, Public Record Office, London.

9.9 Feminist critique of the Beveridge Report

Feminist criticism of the Beveridge Report focused on its treatment of married women, especially for reducing them to the status of dependants.

It is where the [Beveridge] Plan falls short of being really national in character, where it shuts out or exempts from all direct participation over nine million adult women ... that it fails and is open to criticism.... The error ... lies in denying to the married woman ... an independent personal status. From this error springs a crop of injustices....

Any plea urging the difficulty of bringing the married woman inside the strict rules of insurance is rebutted by the Plan itself. Where women are concerned the ordinary rules of insurance are honoured more in the breach than in the observance by the sequestration of their premiums when they marry, by the possible exemption of a woman worker ... because she is married, by giving a married woman worker lower benefits for the full contribution, by cutting the fully paid-up pension of a married woman worker when her husband retires, and by various limitations upon women's right to insurance based on purely personal considerations....

It must be emphasised, then, that it is not upon the denial of equal economic status to women that the Plan comes to grief.... It is with the denial of any personal status to a woman because she is married, the denial of her independent personality within marriage, that everything goes wrong....

Far from putting a premium on marriage, as it purports to do, the Plan penalises both the married woman and marriage itself.... The new proposal is that every woman on marriage shall lose her accumulated payments ... and cease to be an insured person. Should she remain in work or take fresh work, she has to requalify for insurance....

The report generally argues that the married woman does not need the same benefits, and in particular that she is not responsible for the payment of rent. This is to confuse the principles of Insurance with those of Assistance....

This Memorandum has dealt with what is considered to be a basic failure in the Plan; the failure to treat women as full and independent fellow citizens with men....

The average working housewife must, if there is to be any reality in an insurance scheme, be looked upon as a gainfully occupied partner, in that her contribution to the home has a definite financial value, and inasmuch as her work there is as much her livelihood as the work of those put into Class II of the scheme. It is true that under the present law the married woman has no right to any penny of the husband's income; nevertheless she has the right to subsistence (of which a suitable insurance contribution might well form a part)....

Practically all the disabilities and anomalies criticised could have been obviated had there been a different approach to the whole subject. At present the Plan is mainly a man's plan for man.

Elizabeth Abbott and Katherine Bompas, *The Woman Citizen and Social Security*, London, 1943, pp. 3–4, 6, 19, 20.

9.10 Feminists versus Beveridge

A conference of women's organisations on the Beveridge scheme objected to the way it treated women and urged that it be revised to incorporate the following changes.

The following are the recommendations made [by the conference]:
1. The same retirement age for men and women.

131

2. The safeguarding of pension and other rights of unpaid domestic workers by compulsory insurance on their behalf.

3. Direct insurance of the married woman – the housewife – with benefits adjusted to her needs, including cash benefit when disabled by sickness or accident and retirement pension at the normal age.

4. Maintenance of a woman's insurance rights on marriage, subject to general tests of genuine desire and availability for work.

5. No exemption from insurance of the married woman worker save the general exemption for any person earning less than £75 a year.

6. Full normal benefit for the insured woman worker when unemployed or disabled.

7. Full pension in her own right for the insured married woman.

8. Payment by the single woman of an equal contribution for equal benefit.

9. Removal of all moral tests, especially as applied to women only.

10. Widowhood benefit to be recognised as and called Temporary Loss of Livelihood Benefit.

11. Maternity Grant to be adequate and this and Maternity Benefit to be recognised for what they are, not individual benefits but Family Benefits designed to safeguard the bearing and rearing of children.

12. The inclusion of the unmarried wife and mother in insurance on a normal and fair basis, entitling her to share in these family benefits, including guardianship benefit.

It was agreed to press the demands on the Government by following the procedure adopted in the Equal Compensation Campaign, that is to form an ad hoc Committee of Women's organisations under the chairmanship of a woman M.P.

'Conference on the Proposals in the Beveridge Report as They Affect Women', *The Women's Bulletin* (journal of the Women's Freedom League), 12 November 1943, p. 1.

9.11   Cabinet discussion of the white paper

Opponents of reform within the Cabinet attempted to postpone the social insurance white paper by stressing the uncertainty of postwar economic conditions.

The War Cabinet had a general discussion of our post-war financial commitments, in the course of which it was pointed out that to a very considerable extent the social security scheme and other plans for improving the standard of life were dependent on building up a satisfactory volume of export trade after the war. It was also urged that there was need for caution in accepting any fresh financial commitments until we could see our way clearly through the grave difficulties of the post-war period....

The main point dealt with in discussion was whether parts I and II of the draft White Paper should be presented to Parliament forthwith, with a view to debates in both Houses before the Recess.

War Cabinet minute, 4 July 1944, CAB 65/43, WM (44) 87, Public Record Office, London.

9.12   White paper on social insurance

The white paper was entitled *Social Insurance* to signal that the government was endorsing a limited insurance scheme rather than the open-ended social security plan Beveridge proposed. It thus differed from the Beveridge scheme in several respects, including rejecting Beveridge's proposals for subsistence-level benefits and unlimited unemployment benefit.

In the result the Government are now in a position to put forward their proposals for a new scheme of social insurance.... The cost of these family allowances will be met wholly from the proceeds of taxation; they are thus outside the bounds of the scheme of social insurance.... With that one exception, the Government have adhered to the principle that freedom from want must be achieved in the first instance by social insurance – that benefits must be earned by contributions.

8. The Government have also decided that the scope of social insurance should be extended in two different senses – the range and amount of benefit provided and the number of people included.... The scheme as a whole will embrace, not certain occupations and income groups, but the entire population....

9. Certain other general principles have been adopted in framing the policy set out in the following pages. There has been no attempt to vary contributions with the earnings of those who make them: broadly the principle adopted has been that of equal benefits for equal contributions....

12. In fixing the rates of benefit to be provided under the scheme the Government have considered whether it would be practicable to adopt a subsistence basis for benefits. In the debates of February, 1943, they expressed the preliminary view that it was not practicable and further examination of the question has confirmed this view....

13. Benefits must be paid for, and a high level of benefit must mean a high level of contribution. The Government therefore conclude that the right objective is a rate of benefit which provides a reasonable insurance against want and at the same time takes account of the maximum contribution which the great body of contributors can properly be asked to bear. There still remains the individual's opportunity to achieve for himself ... a standard of comfort and amenity which is no part of a compulsory scheme of social insurance to provide. And in reserve there must remain a scheme of National Assistance designed to fill the inevitable gaps left by insurance and to supplement it where ... necessary....

50. The following proposals [for family allowances] are based upon two principles, first that nothing should be done to remove from parents the responsibility of maintaining their children, and second that it is in the national interest for the State to help parents to discharge that responsibility properly. The scheme here set out is not intended to provide full maintenance for each child. It is rather a general contribution to the needs of families with children.

51. The purpose of such a scheme can best be attained if a substantial part of the benefit is given in kind. The school meals and milk services will therefore be extended to make them available to pupils in primary and secondary schools in receipt of grant from the Ministry of Education or the Scottish Education Department. These benefits in kind will be free of cost to the parents....

53. In the absence of special circumstances (such as divorce or separation) the order for the payment of the allowance will be

made out in favour of the father as the normal economic head of the household....

67. The [Beveridge] Report recommended that both sickness and unemployment benefit should be unlimited in duration.... As already announced in Parliament, the Government cannot accept this recommendation....

84. The proposal in the [Beveridge] Report was that the rate of pension to be payable twenty years from the start of the scheme would be fixed now, at 40s. (joint) and 24s. (single)....

85. The Government have already announced that they cannot accept these [pension] proposals ... and that, in their view, it is preferable that the new standard rate of pension ... should be payable from the time the new scheme comes into effect....

106. The last census showed that seven married women out of eight were not in gainful occupation. Their primary need is, therefore, support when their husbands' earnings are interrupted by sickness or loss of employment; and there are special needs in connection with maternity. The Government propose to cover these needs and to relate the benefits substantially to the husbands' position in insurance....

107. In a minority of cases a woman re-enters or remains in employment after her marriage. Her position is then, in many respects, a special one....

108. On marriage a woman insured before her marriage will be required to choose whether to be insured in her own right ... or to be exempt and rely on her husband's insurance....

118. The Government have considered whether there should be ... a temporary separation benefit (akin to the benefit provided on the death of a husband) where, through no fault of her own, a wife loses maintenance to which she is entitled from her husband.... The Government feel that the question whether loss of maintenance is the fault of the wife is not one which should be determined by a Department responsible for administering the social insurance scheme. The wife must seek other remedies open to her to secure maintenance....

120. Maternity grant, maternity benefit and attendant's allowance will be available to single women on the same terms as for married, except that title will rest on the woman's own insurance....

159. It has been stated that when the new insurance scheme is in operation there will be in reserve the National Assistance

scheme to meet the requirements of the specially necessitous case. The Government propose that the scope of National Assistance ... should be extended to include financial assistance to all on proof of need....

161. The Government ... attach great importance to the preservation of the distinction between insurance and assistance, and it is proposed to retain in the final arrangements separate administration for Social Insurance and National Assistance.

Social Insurance, Cmd 6550, London, 1944, pp. 6–7, 14–15, 17, 21–2, 26, 28–9, 35–6.

9.13   The white paper: a Conservative document?

> Although some Conservatives feared they were being drawn into support for a Labour reform programme, shrewd insiders such as Butler, Conservative MP and Minister of Education, recognised that the social insurance white paper was significantly closer to the Conservative Party's position than to Beveridge's original scheme.

If the Conservative element had been any more outspoken than it was recently over the Town and Country Planning Bill, no central reconstruction policy would have emerged from the committee at all!...

Similarly on the Beveridge Report, the final document [white paper] stresses the features of thrift and gets back to placing the whole Beveridge scheme upon an insurance or a subsistence basis. Conservatives in the country will prefer this attitude to that which Beveridge adopted.

R. A. Butler to Lord Woolton (Minister of Reconstruction), 13 September 1944, Lord Woolton papers, ms Woolton 16, f. 9, Bodleian Library, Oxford.

10
Family allowances and the National Health Service

The 1945 Family Allowances Act provided a payment of 5s weekly to the mother for each child after the first. The Act was not due to evacuation-prompted concern over child poverty; policy makers were more concerned with stimulating the birth rate and maintaining the 'less eligibility' principle. Although both coalition parties supported a national health service, they differed profoundly over what form it should take. The 1945 Conservative government was so dissatisfied with the 1944 national health service white paper that it drafted a new white paper outlining the very different health service the Conservative Party intended to introduce if it won the 1945 general election.

10.1 Conservative case for family allowances

By the early years of the war Conservative support for family allowances was increasing, in part because they were presented as a solution to the problem of the declining rate of population growth.

Even where wages allow for at any rate enough food, a large family means a serious lowering of the standard of life and the prospects of individual children.

The result is a steady shrinkage of family life. Our birthrate is already 20 per cent below replacement level. How a shrinking population is to provide a home market for our industries or the revenues to sustain our defence is a problem which may call for much bolder measures than anything proposed at this moment. Family Allowances may do something to check the decline.

Leo Amery (Conservative MP and a leading Conservative proponent of family allowances) to Arthur Greenwood (Labour MP and member of the War Cabinet), 18 January 1941, PIN 8/163, Public Record Office, London.

137

10.2 Rationale for family allowances

As wartime prices rose, advocates were quick to present family allowances as an economically preferable alternative to a general wage increase.

[Wing Commander Wright speaking for Leo Amery]: I think you will agree that a very large section of the public was profoundly shocked, if I said rocked I do not think it would be using too strong a term, by the conditions which were revealed in the evacuation of 1939 and the conditions in which a very large number of our own future citizens are being brought up, and I think we must very largely relate that to the fact that today at the lowest end of the scale the married man with a family has to bear a financial burden which is altogether out of all proportion greater, if he has children, than a married man who has no family to bring up or a single man.... My third, and perhaps most important, point is I fail to see how any Minister can justify the granting of comparatively substantial family child allowances to the wealthiest members of the country and at the same time entirely deny it to those at the poorest end of the scale who, after all, are the people who require these allowances more than anyone else. I refer of course to the incidence of the child allowances on the Income Tax.... I do not see how it is possible really to justify the state of affairs where a man with £10,000 a year gets approximately 10s a week for every child he has got but a man who is so unfortunate that he is getting less than £4 a week gets practically nothing at all.... Summing up it seems to me that we have to make up our minds whether it is desirable for the future of our Empire that children should be born and whether they are National assets....

Miss Rathbone: ... Thirdly, think of the impossibility of meeting that varying incidence of child responsibility otherwise than through family allowances without increasing the inflationary tendency which is already alarming a number of people.... Either you must raise wages so that they are enough to provide for a mythical average family or better still your largest family that anybody has, and thereby provide for the number of imaginary children or you must provide for the children that already exist. The system of trying to provide for these children through wages given everyone is like dealing with a shower of incendiary bombs on one part of London by sprinkling the whole of London equally.

Chancellor of the Exchequer [Kingsley Wood]: What I am doubtful about in fact is whether if the Chancellor of the Exchequer has £100,000,000 it would not be [better] used for improvements in the medical services or in education or in the further provision of free and cheap milk and school meals and so on; where the money that was spent was sure in fact to reach the recipients ... can you in fact be sure when you give payments of this kind that they will reach the children?

Notes of a meeting of the Chancellor of Exchequer and MPs on family allowances, 16 June 1941, PIN 8/163, Public Record Office, London.

10.3 Family allowances: pros and cons

At the above 16 June meeting with MPs urging family allowances, the Chancellor of the Exchequer agreed to prepare a white paper. But the document he issued undercut the case for family allowances by repeatedly suggesting that children would benefit more from additional spending on child welfare schemes than from family allowances. Reformers were also disappointed to discover the Chancellor intended to restrict the scheme to lower-income groups by the use of a means test.

2. It will be generally conceded that proposals in regard to family allowances form part of a big social question, including the question whether the assumption of further responsibility by the State for the welfare of children should take the form of assistance to the parents in cash or direct provision in kind. Those who advocate a system of allowances hold not only that State assistance towards the welfare of children should be extended, but that the extension should take the particular form of an addition in cash to the incomes of parents. The various considerations which have been put forward by different advocates of a system of family allowances are in general well known. They include particularly the following:–

139

(i) the effect of family allowances in lessening the risk of malnutrition (with consequential deleterious results upon health, efficiency and well-being) in the case of large families;

(ii) the difficulty of putting the parents of large families into a position to meet the increased cost of living by means of increased wages without increasing wages all round, and so setting up an inflationary movement;

(iii) the possible influence of family allowances in encouraging parenthood and therefore in counteracting the decline in the national birth rate;

(iv) the fact that income tax relief is given in respect of children whose parents are liable to income tax; it is held that parents not so liable ought to receive a similar benefit by way of cash allowance....

4. There are, on the other hand, as is well-known, those who have doubted the expediency of family allowances and who have not been convinced that they can be introduced without affecting detrimentally collective bargaining in industry and without prejudicing wage negotiations. It is also thought by some that, on account of their cost, family allowances would absorb funds which would otherwise be available for further development of other Social Services, some of which might be thought to demand priority. Those who hold this view consider that the welfare of children can best be promoted by developments, such as improved housing and increased educational and health services, which can only be provided collectively. As in the case of the considerations put forward by those who are in favour of family allowances, no attempt is made in this memorandum to set out in detail the views that have been expressed from time to time by those who doubt the expediency of introducing allowances or to assess the validity of their arguments.

5. Even if there is now thought to be a sufficient measure of agreement as to the desirability of such a scheme, consideration would have to be given to the budgetary and economic reactions of expenditure on the scale that would be involved, and the question would also arise whether, if further expenditure on social services should be possible, it should be incurred on family allowances or on other services in respect of which there are demands for extensions and improvements....

10. By a non-contributory scheme is meant one financed by general taxation. The first question that arises is whether all classes should benefit by such a scheme, or whether it should be restricted to particular classes, and if so, how the scope of the scheme should be defined. If the object of the scheme is to safeguard the larger families against financial hardship, it should be confined to persons of limited means. Thus, the scope of the scheme might be limited (a) by an income test....

'Family allowances: memorandum by the Chancellor of the Exchequer', May 1942, *Parliamentary Papers 1941–42*, vol. 9, Cmd 6354, London, 1942.

10.4   Cabinet opposition to reform

Within the Cabinet the Chancellor of the Exchequer, Kingsley Wood, led the opposition to family allowances, but he was backed by other powerful ministers, including R. A. Butler and Ernest Bevin.

The Chancellor [of the Exchequer] added that he did not think it necessary to deal at the moment with the merits of the proposal which had been made. He thought, however, it was open to debate whether the payment in cash of allowances at the rate of, say, 5s a week would in fact afford a proper solution of the question, or be in conformity with the present Government policy. It was also arguable whether, assuming that we had £10 millions or £20 millions a year to spend on children, they would derive most benefit if this sum was used to pay Family Allowances in cash or expended in other ways.

The Minister of Labour and National Service [Bevin] also expressed doubts as to the value of allowances paid in cash.

The President of the Board of Education [Butler] said that inquiries made of his senior Divisional Inspectors showed that many of them believed that direct monetary grants would not be used, at any rate wholly, for the benefit of the children. He would like to see any available money spent on the provision of free meals for school children (at present only a small proportion of the school children receiving school meals had them without payment), free milk (at present milk was free only for the small proportion of necessitous children out of the total of three-quarters of the school population receiving it), the provision of clothing (which would be a new service) and free medical treatment.

Lord President's Committee minute, 2 June 1942, CAB, 71/6, LP (42) 34, Public Record Office, London.

10.5   Beveridge and family allowances

> The government accepted 'children's allowances' after Beveridge recommended them in his report. His argument for the allowances emphasised their importance in maintaining the 'less eligibility' principle – that is, the lowest-paid employed man should be better off than if he were unemployed.

410. The first of three assumptions underlying the Plan for Social Security is a general scheme of children's allowances. This means that direct provision for the maintenance of dependent children will be made by payment of allowances to those responsible for the care of those children. The assumption rests on two connected arguments.

411. First, it is unreasonable to seek to guarantee an income sufficient for subsistence, while earnings are interrupted by unemployment or disability, without ensuring sufficient income during earning. Social insurance should be a part of a policy of a national minimum. But a national minimum for families of every size cannot in practice be secured by a wage system, which must be based on the product of a man's labour and not on the size of his family. The social surveys of Britain between the two wars show that in the first thirty years of this century real wages rose by about one-third without reducing want to insignificance, and that the want which remained was almost wholly due to two causes – interruption or loss of earning power and large families.

412. Second, it is dangerous to allow benefit during unemployment or disability to equal or exceed earnings during work. But, without allowances for children, during earning and not-earning alike, this danger cannot be avoided. It has been experienced in an appreciable number of cases under unemployment benefit and unemployment assistance in the past. The

maintenance of employment – last and most important of the three assumptions of social security – will be impossible without greater fluidity of labour and other resources in the aftermath of war than has been achieved in the past. To secure this, the gap between income during earning and during interruption of earning should be kept as large as possible for every man. It cannot be kept large for men with large families, except either by making their benefit in unemployment and disability inadequate, or by giving allowances for children in time of earning and not-earning alike.

Social Insurance and Allied Services, Cmd 6404, London, 1942, p. 154.

10.6   Allowances paid to the mother?

> Once agreement had been reached that family allowances should be introduced, controversy continued over whether they should be paid to the mother or the father.

The Secretary of State for Foreign Affairs [Anthony Eden] informed the War Cabinet that the Minister of Social Insurance and he had received that day a deputation representing all political Parties, which had pressed very strongly that the Family Allowances Bill should be amended so as to provide that the allowances should 'belong' to the mother. There was reason to think that this claim would be widely supported in the forthcoming Debate in the House of Commons. The deputation had suggested that this was a question which might properly be left for decision by a free vote of the House.

In discussion the following points were made:–

(a) The Reconstruction Committee had considered this question at length, and had decided that either parent should be able to cash the allowance. The White Paper had proceeded on this basis; but the Committee had been advised that for the purposes of legal title it was necessary to provide in the Bill that the allowance 'belonged' either to the father or the mother. They had decided that the legal title should be with the father. In reaching this decision they had been influenced mainly by two considerations. First, under the general law, the father was responsible for the maintenance of the child; and there would be grave difficulties in reconciling with this general principle of the law a provision giving the mother the legal title to this particular allowance. Secondly, the allowance was intended to supplement the family income, not to provide in full for the needs of the child. To give the legal title to the mother might imply a recognition that she was responsible for the child's maintenance, and might thus provide a demand for an increase in the allowance sufficient to enable her to discharge that responsibility in full.

(b) It was argued, on the other hand, that in practice the mother was normally responsible for the household budget and the welfare of the children, and that on this account she should have control of the allowance. The general sense of public opinion would be sympathetic towards giving the mother a right to the allowance.

(c) The War Cabinet were informed that the Labour Party were likely to move an amendment to substitute 'women' for 'men' in the relevant Clause of the Bill. It was generally agreed that it would be unfortunate if this question became an issue between the two main political Parties....

The War Cabinet –

Agreed that in the Debate on the Second Reading of the Family Allowances Bill the Government spokesman should announce that on this point the decision would be left to a free vote of the House, but at the appropriate stage the Attorney General would advise the House on the legal issues involved before the question was put to the vote.

War Cabinet minute, 6 March 1945, CAB 65/49, WM (45) 26, Public Record Office, London.

10.7   Rathbone on payment to the mother

Eleanor Rathbone initiated the campaign for family allowances some 25 years earlier as a means of recognising the value of mothers' work. Proposing that the allowances be paid to the fathers thus fundamentally altered the reform.

What will happen if the House allows this proposal to go through unchanged? The Government have decided to leave it to a free vote of the House. I am glad of that, but I would rather they should decide at once, because I realise perfectly well that they have blundered into this decision: it was not a stroke of Machiavellian policy to degrade the status of motherhood. But the Cabinet is composed of men, and they cannot be expected to realise how women think on this question. I want to warn them of the intensity of women's feelings about it.... But the women's organisations are already planning to make sure that every politically-conscious woman in the country knows at the next election how her representative has voted. I took part in that long bitter struggle for women's vote before the last war.... But I do not want to go through all that again. It was a bitter struggle, and it caused very ugly results.... Do we want this sex grievance to raise its ugly head at the next General Election...? Do not force us back into what we thought we had done with – an era of sex antagonism.

If the Bill goes through in its present form I cannot vote for the Third Reading, although I worked for this thing for over 25 years. It would be one of the bitterest disappointments of my political life if the Bill did not go through. But I foresee too well the consequences if it goes through in a form which practically throws an insult in the faces of those to whom the country owes most, the actual or potential mothers, whom this country needs so badly if we are not to fall into the status of a second-rate Power.... I beg Members to take their responsibilities seriously, and to think again, to beware how they encourage sex antagonism – which we once thought was dead – to become once more an issue in a General Election.

Eleanor Rathbone, *Hansard, Parliamentary Debates*, fifth series, vol. 408, 8 March 1945, cc. 2282–3.

10.8 Churchill and family allowances

Family allowances drew support for very different reasons, but Churchill continued to view the reform as a contribution to population policy.

I see today in 'The Times', that the [Family Allowances] Bill empowers the Ministers to reduce or withhold allowances payable to the families of Service men and women. Considering that the object in view is to encourage the birth and nourishment of children, I cannot see why this additional benefit should be denied to those classes.

Winston Churchill to John Anderson (Chancellor of the Exchequer), 9 March 1945, PREM 4/89/7, Public Record Office, London.

10.9   Family allowances and wages

> Despite Churchill's continued linking of family allowances with population policy, the Chancellor of the Exchequer defended the reform as a means of avoiding inflationary wage increases.

2. There are substantial grounds for withholding family allowances under the Bill from members of the Services. Family allowances have been advocated primarily as a corrective of the civilian wage system, in which the amount of a man's remuneration depends on the value of his labour and not on the size of his family. This must be the basis of a wage structure in a society in which there is private enterprise, and employers have to take profit and loss into account. But it has the disadvantage that a wage which is sufficient for a single man or childless couple may involve hardship and even want where a large family depends on a single wage earner.

Chancellor of Exchequer to the Prime Minister, 14 March 1945, PREM 4/89/7, Public Record Office, London.

10.10   Public attitudes toward a proposed national health service

> Although public opinion strongly supported the creation of a national health service, the percentage in favour among the higher-income group was considerably less than for the rest of the population.

Question: Do you think that a State-run medical service would, or would not, be beneficial to the nation as a whole?

	Yes	No	Don't know
	%	%	%
Total:	70	17	13
Men	73	16	11
Women	68	17	15
Age groups:			
21–29	71	14	15
30–49	71	18	11
50 and over	68	17	15
Economic groups:			
Higher	56	32	12
Middle	70	22	8
Lower	71	14	15

Spontaneous reasons given for choice
  In favour
    1. It would do away with preferential treatment. Specialist medical attention would then be available for all, and everybody would benefit. The poorer classes in particular would get treatment that they cannot now afford.
  Against
    1. We've had enough of panels. Private patients are better looked after.
    2. It is better to have competition. State services are unsatisfactory.

'Opinion on state-run medical service', Home Intelligence report, 8 July 1943, INF 1/292, Public Record Office, London.

10.11   Cabinet discussion of the white paper

Because of the strong differences of opinion within the Cabinet, it decided to publish the white paper as a consultative document rather than as reflecting the agreed views of the government.

The Minister of Reconstruction [Lord Woolton] explained the scheme and admitted that there had been 'differences of opinion on a number of points'. Points in discussion were:
  (a) The scheme did not involve the abolition of a private medical practice. Although the public service would provide free

147

medical treatment for all who cared to avail themselves of it, it would be inexpedient to prevent those who desired from making private arrangements for treatment. Equally it would have been wrong to exclude any class of persons from treatment under the public service merely on the ground that they could afford to pay for treatment as private patients.

(b) It must be recognized that the scheme would constitute some threat to private medical practice – any proposals for the establishment of a comprehensive medical service must have that effect. On the other hand, it was pointed out that the proposals for grouped practice – whether in health centres or otherwise – were likely to lead to increased efficiency among the rank and file of the medical profession.

(c) The suggestion was made that the scheme would involve the establishment of a large bureaucratic machine which, through the proposed Central Medical Board, would determine where each doctor would practice. It was pointed out that, if there was a shortage of doctors and the State had undertaken to provide a universal service, the State must have some power to control the general distribution of doctors in the public service. The degree of this control was not, however, so drastic as had been suggested. In the case of separate practice, for example, all that was proposed was that the consent of the Board should be required before a vacant public practice was filled or a new public practice established; and it was intended that this consent should be withheld only if there were enough or too many doctors in the area.

(d) It was suggested that the scheme was likely to meet with keen opposition from the doctors, and would be represented as undermining the whole basis of the medical profession. The War Cabinet were informed that, while opinion among doctors might be divided, it was likely that the scheme would be supported by a substantial proportion of the profession....

The Prime Minister asked that in presenting their scheme to the public, Ministers should stress the fact that it did not represent the final views of the Government; that it was put forward for public discussion and that constructive criticism would be welcomed; that, when there had been an opportunity for the formation of public opinion, the details would be further discussed with the medical profession and other interests affected;

and that only then would the Government proceed in the light of all these discussions to formulate their final conclusions and to bring forward proposals for legislation.

War Cabinet minute, 9 February 1944, CAB 65/41, WM (44) 17, Public Record Office, London.

10.12 Conservative resistance to the white paper

At the request of Conservatives who opposed the white paper, Churchill asked that its publication be suspended in order to provide an opportunity for it to be reshaped in a more Conservative cast.

Publication of the White Paper on the National Health Service is being suspended, as you desire.

I assume that you want time for further consideration of the view put forward at the War Cabinet by the Minister of Information. If so, I think I should let you know the political difficulties as I see them.

The Government have already accepted in principle the idea of a National Medical Service or National Health Service. They committed themselves to that in the Debates on the Beveridge Report in 1942. If you are to have a national service, I am satisfied that you will not get one which is more acceptable to the Conservative point of view, and more economical of public money, than the scheme which has been thrashed out by the Reconstruction Committee.

As I said last night, this is a compromise scheme: but it is a compromise which is very much more favourable to the Conservatives than to the Labour Ministers; and, when it is published, I should expect more criticism from the Left than from Conservative circles. My difficulty on the Committee has been to persuade the Labour Ministers to accept a scheme which fell so far short of their desire for a State salaried service; and I had great trouble in persuading the Labour Ministers at the last moment to refrain from criticizing the scheme at the War Cabinet on that ground.

If discussion of the whole scheme is to be reopened – particularly if it is known or believed, that this is being done to meet the views of Conservative Ministers – I fear that the Labour Ministers may withdraw their support of the scheme and stand out for something more drastic which would be far more repugnant to Conservative feeling.

Lord Woolton to Winston Churchill, 10 February 1944, CAB 124/244, Public Record Office, London.

10.13   Cabinet conflict on the white paper

During the Cabinet discussion of the white paper there were strong differences of opinion along party lines.

The following were the main points raised in the course of a further discussion of the scheme outlined in the White Paper:–

(a) Would the scheme mean the end of private medical practice and the family doctor?

The War Cabinet were informed that the scheme would not prevent the continuance of private practice; in particular, doctors taking part in the public service would not be prevented from taking private patients. Nor would it affect the relation between the doctor and the patient. The conception of the family doctor would indeed be strengthened, since dependants of insured persons would in future be eligible for free medical treatment.

It was true that the eventual effect of the scheme might be to limit the scope for private medical practice – since, when free medical treatment was available for all, there might be some reduction in the numbers willing to pay for private treatment. At the same time, the scheme would not directly prohibit or restrict the extent of private medical practice.

(b) Would the scheme mean the end of the voluntary hospitals, which had for so long taken the lead in teaching and research?

These hospitals, supported by voluntary contributions, were rightly jealous of their independence. Could they continue to play the same part in the development of medical science if they became financially dependent on public authorities and had, in consequence, to accept public control?

The War Cabinet were informed that it was not proposed that the management of the voluntary hospitals should be taken over by public authority. The scheme contemplated that these hospitals should make a certain number of beds available for public patients, and that they should be paid for this service....

(c) To what extent would the scheme interfere with the right of doctors to set up in practice as consultants?

It was explained that the proposals for a consultants' service, linked with the hospitals, would make the service available to a far wider range of patients. The eventual result of the scheme would be to increase the number of consultants, and to improve their distribution over the country as a whole. This would be brought about, not by any system of state selection of doctors for consultant work, but by providing greater opportunities for doctors to practise as consultants. The scheme would not, however, prevent consultants from seeing patients privately, in addition to any part which they took in the public medical service.

War Cabinet minute, 15 February 1944, CAB 65/41, WM (44) 21, Public Record Office, London.

10.14 White paper on a national health service

> While expressing the government's commitment to some type of national health service, the white paper left unresolved basic issues as to the nature of the service.

The main reason for change is that the Government believe that, at this stage of social development, the care of personal health should be put on a new footing and be made available to everybody as a publicly sponsored service. Just as people are accustomed to look to public organisation for essential facilities like a clean and safe water supply or good highways, accepting these as things which the community combines to provide for the benefit of the individual without distinction or section or group, so they should be able to look for proper facilities for the care of their personal health to a publicly organised service available to all who want to use it – a service for which all would be paying as taxpayers and ratepayers and contributors to some national scheme of social insurance.

In spite of the substantial progress of many years and the many good services built up under public authority and by private effort, it is still not true to say that everyone can get all the kinds of medical and hospital service which he or she may require. Whether people can do so still depends too much upon circumstance, upon where they happen to live or work, to what group (e.g. of age, or vocation) they happen to belong, or what happens to be the matter with them. Nor is the care of health yet wholly divorced from ability to pay for it, although great progress has already been made in eliminating the financial barrier to obtaining most of the essential services. There is not yet, in short, a comprehensive cover for health provided for all people alike. This is what it is now the Government's intention to provide.

To take one very important example, the first-line care of health for everyone requires a personal doctor or a family doctor, a general medical practitioner available for consultation on all problems of health and sickness. At present, the National Health Insurance scheme makes this provision for a large number of people; but it does not give it to the wives and the children and the dependants....

When a hospital's services are needed, it is far from true that everyone can get all that is required. Here it is not so much a question of people not being eligible to get the services which they need, as a matter of the practical distribution of those services. The hospital and specialist services have grown up without a national or even an area plan. In one area there may be already established a variety of hospitals. Another area, although the need is there, may be sparsely served. One hospital may have a long waiting list and be refusing admission to cases which another hospital not far away could suitably accommodate and treat at once....

Nor should there be any compulsion into the service, either for the patient or for the doctor. The basis must be that the new service will be there for everyone who wants it – and indeed will be so designed that it can be looked upon as the normal method by which people get all the advice and help which they want; but if anyone prefers not to use it, or likes to make private arrangements outside the service, he must be at liberty to do so. Similarly, if any medical practitioner prefers not to take part in the new service and to rely wholly on private work outside it, he must also be at liberty to do so.

The proposed service must be 'comprehensive' in two senses – first, that it is available to all people and, second, that it covers all necessary forms of health care....

The arrangements for general medical practice in the comprehensive service – i.e. for ensuring a personal or family doctor for everybody – present the most difficult problem of all....

If the service is to be free to the people for whom it is provided, the doctors taking part in it will look to the public funds for their remuneration. They must, therefore, be in some contractual relationship with public authority, which in turn must be able to attach such conditions as will ensure that the services which the people get are the services which they need (and for which they will be paying in taxation and otherwise) and that they can get them where and when they need them. The State must, therefore, take a greater part in future in regard to general medical practice.

The method of embodying general medical practice in a national service must observe two principles. The first, which mainly concerns the patient, is that people must be able to choose for themselves the doctor from whom they wish to seek their medical advice and treatment, and to change to another doctor if they so wish. Freedom of choice is not absolute now; it depends on the number and accessibility of doctors and on the fact that there is a limit to the load which any one doctor can or should take on. But the present degree of freedom must not be generally diminished, and the fact that public organisation ensures the service must not destroy the sense of choice and personal association which is at the heart of 'family' doctoring. The second principle, which mainly concerns the doctor, is that the practice of medicine is an individual and personal art, impatient of regimentation. Whatever the organisation, the doctors taking part must remain free to direct their clinical knowledge and personal skill for the benefit of their patients in the way which they feel to be best.

One method would be to abandon entirely the present system, on which National Health Insurance has been based, and to substitute for it a system under which all doctors taking part would become the direct employees of the State or of local authorities and would be remunerated by salary. As a problem of administration, there would be no insuperable difficulty in organising a scheme of this kind. But this is a highly controversial question, on which opinions are sharply divided. Many experienced and skilled doctors would be unwilling to take part in a service so conceived. They would hold that it infringed the second of the two principles just stated, and that if they became the salaried servants whether of the State or of local authorities, they would lose their professional freedom and be fettered in the exercise of their individual skill. Other doctors, with an equal right to be heard, would welcome a salaried service, believing that it would relieve them from business anxieties and enable them to devote themselves more freely to the practice of their profession. Lay opinion is similarly varied.

The Government have approached the question solely from the point of view of what is needed to make the new service efficient. Some of the proposals made in this Paper involve forms of medical practice for which present methods of payment are inappropriate, if not unworkable. Where this is so, remuneration by salary or its equivalent is suggested. A universal change to a salaried system is not, however, in the Government's view, necessary to the efficiency of the service....

The conception of grouped practice finds its most usual expression in the idea, advocated by the Medical Planning Commission and others, of conducting practice in specially designed and equipped premises where the group can collaborate and share up-to-date resources – the idea of the 'Health Centre'. The Government ... intend, therefore, to design the new service so as to give scope to a full trial of this new method of organising medical practice....

But there is one important question in regard to the method of remuneration of the doctor, when practising in co-operation with a group of colleagues in a Health Centre, which does not arise in the same way when he is in separate practice outside. That is the method of payment of the individual doctor.

It seems fundamental that inside a Centre the grouped doctors should not be in financial competition for patients....

There is therefore a strong case for basing future practice in a Health Centre on a salaried remuneration or on some similar alternative which will not involve mutual competition within the Centre.

'A national health service', *Parliamentary Papers 1943–44*, vol. 8, Cmd 6502, London, 1944, pp. 6–7, 9, 26–7, 30–2.

10.15   The 1945 national health service white paper

The 1945 Conservative caretaker government prepared a new white paper on a national health service which differed in important respects from the coalition government's white paper. They did not, however, publish it, for fear that it would be taken as evidence that the Conservative Party was seeking to weaken the new health service.

The following arguments were advanced against the publication of the White Paper before the Election....

(d) Objections would be raised in Parliament if the White Paper were presented so late in the session that there was no opportunity for debate. If, on the other hand, it were presented earlier and time were found for a debate, the Opposition might make damaging criticism on some points at which the original plan had been modified – e.g. it would be alleged that under the new proposals the Health Centre experiment would be crippled, and that there would be no means of securing an efficient distribution of general practitioners throughout the country.

(e) Apart from a debate in Parliament, Opposition speakers would make play with the same points during the Election. It was true that the modifications now proposed would go far to meet the views of the doctors, local authorities and voluntary hospitals; but it was not clear that they would be equally acceptable to the general public as a whole. Some of the changes would be represented by Opposition speakers as likely to provide a less efficient service for the general public....

(g) If this White Paper were published, it would be widely represented as cutting down the proposals in the earlier White Paper presented by the Coalition Government. The suggestion would be made that the Conservative Party had taken advantage of the break-up of the Coalition to withdraw their support from proposals which had been put forward by the Coalition Government.

Meeting of Cabinet ministers chaired by Lord Woolton, 6 June 1945, MH 77/30A, Public Record Office, London.

10.16   The Conservative proposal for a health service

The 1945 Conservative government's scheme gave the medical profession much greater control over the proposed health service, weakened state control of the voluntary hospitals, and reduced the role proposed for health centres.

The Health Ministers sought authority to announce these changes in general terms, before the Election, and to state that it was the Government's intention to introduce legislation early in the new Parliament to give effect to the modified scheme.

The Minister of Health said that if no such announcement were made, it would be alleged that the present Government intended to withhold or delay the introduction of a National Health Service. In fact, substantial progress had been made in the discussions with the interested parties, and the modified scheme was likely to command a large measure of support from doctors, local authorities (except the London County Council) and voluntary hospitals. The original scheme had included a number of features which had aroused opposition from the interested parties, and it was desirable to make it clear before the Election that the present Government were prepared to modify these features of the plan. It was undesirable that candidates supporting the Government should be left in the position of having to defend at the Election those proposals in the original White Paper which the Health Ministers were now prepared to modify.

In reply to questions raised in the discussion, the Minister of Health said that the main changes now proposed could be broadly described under six heads. First, the planning of the health services would be shared between the local authorities and experts representing both the hospitals and the doctors. Second, there would be regional advisory bodies based on the wider areas influenced by the medical schools of the universities. Third, the local authorities would retain responsibility for the administration of their hospitals, instead of being required to transfer them to Joint Boards. Fourth, there would be no 'direction' of doctors and no central employment of doctors by a Central Medical Board. Fifth, the basis of payments to voluntary hospitals from local public funds would be modified in a way which would become acceptable to the voluntary hospitals. Sixth, the new proposals went beyond those of the original White Paper in the dental and ophthalmic services to be provided and also in the provision of aids for the deaf.

Cabinet minute, 15 June 1945, CAB 65/53, WM (45) 9, Public Record Office, London.

11
Education

The 1944 Education Act is often cited as the most important reform legislation actually introduced during the war. But it achieved neither of the goals reform proponents desired: equality of opportunity and increased technical education. Although the 1938 Spens Report claimed improved technical education was crucial to reviving the British economy, the Act allowed, but did not require, local government to take action. Because it was permissive rather than compulsory, the Act has been described as merely 'an opened gate to an empty construction site on which the local authorities might or might not ... build'.[1]

11.1 Butler and reform

When R. A. Butler, President of the Board of Education, first outlined his proposals for reform to the Prime Minister, he gave priority to the need for improved technical training and for changes in the public schools. The failure of wartime educational reform to achieve either goal partially explains why many historians now view it as a missed opportunity.

I should now like to give you my first impressions of the questions immediately before the Board [of Education].

There is, first, the need for industrial and technical learning and the linking up of schools closely with employment. Secondly, a settlement with the churches about Church schools and religious instruction in schools. Both these questions are nation-wide. Thirdly, there is the question of the future of the Public Schools, which may easily raise widespread controversy.

[1] Correlli Barnett, *The Audit of War*, London, 1986, p. 291.

As regards the first, the country has clearly lagged behind the practice on the Continent and elsewhere....

Then we must try to find a settlement for the Church school question. Neither the Anglican nor Roman Church can find the necessary funds to discharge their statutory duties, and children in voluntary schools are in general at a serious disadvantage as compared with those in Council schools. Any hope of improvement in education will be frustrated unless a durable settlement of this longstanding controversy is reached, though there is no disguising the danger of old antagonisms being raised on this issue.

As for the Public Schools, I hope to have the views of their Governing Bodies before attempting to reach conclusions.

R. A. Butler to the Prime Minister, 12 September 1941, PREM 4/11/6, Public Record Office, London.

11.2 Churchill on educational reform

Opposition from the Prime Minister was one of the obstacles Butler had to overcome in seeking reform.

It would be the greatest mistake to raise the 1902 controversy during the war, and I certainly cannot contemplate a new Education Bill. I think it would also be a great mistake to stir up the Public Schools question at the present time....

We cannot have any Party politics in wartime and both your second and third points raise these in a most acute and dangerous form.

Winston Churchill to R. A. Butler, 13 September 1941, PREM 4/11/6, Public Record Office, London.

11.3 The education white paper

Although the proposal for secondary education for all was an important advance, the requirement that there should be three types of schools, and that religious education should be mandatory, are examples of how the scheme reinforced traditional approaches to education.

1. The Government's purpose in putting forward the reforms described in this Paper is to secure for children a happier childhood and a better start in life; to ensure a fuller measure of education and opportunity for young people and to provide means for all of developing the various talents with which they are endowed and so enriching the inheritance of the country whose citizens they are. The new educational opportunities must not, therefore, be of a single pattern. It is just as important to achieve diversity as it is to ensure equality of educational opportunity.

2. With these ends in view the Government propose to recast the national education service. The new layout is based on a recognition of the principle that education is a continuous process conducted in successive stages. For children below the compulsory school age of 5 there must be a sufficient supply of nursery schools. The period of compulsory school attendance will be extended to 15 without exemptions and with provision for its subsequent extension to 16 as soon as circumstances permit. The period from 5 to leaving age will be divided into two stages, the first, to be known as primary, covering the years up to about 11. After 11 secondary education, of diversified types but of equal standing, will be provided for all children.... The provision of school meals and milk will be made obligatory.

3. When the period of full-time compulsory schooling ends the young person will continue under educational influences up to 18 years of age either by remaining in full-time attendance at a secondary school, or by part-time day attendance at a young people's college.... Opportunities for technical and adult education will be increased.

4. Among other important features of the plan are an effective system of inspection and registration of schools outside the public system; new financial and administrative arrangements for the voluntary schools, and recognition of the special place of religious instruction in school life....

8. There remains one important link to forge between the Public Schools and other analogous schools and the general system. As was indicated in the terms of reference to Lord Fleming's Committee which is inquiring into the question, it is the Government's intention to devise ways and means by which these schools can be more closely associated with the national system....

A system under which fees are charged in one type of post-primary school and prohibited in the other offends against the canon that the nature of a child's education should be determined by his capacity and promise and not by the financial circumstances of his parent....

22. It is intended that the raising of the school leaving age to 15, postponed in 1939, should be brought into effect as soon as possible after the war, but without the arrangements for exemptions made in the 1936 Act, and that provision should be made for a further extension to 16 at a later date....

27. At about the age of 11 comes the change from the junior to the senior stage.... Accordingly, in the future, children at the age of about 11 should be classified, not on the results of a competitive test, but on an assessment of their individual aptitudes largely by such means as school records, supplemented, if necessary, by intelligence tests, due regard being had to their parents' wishes and the careers they have in mind. Even so, the choice of one type of secondary education rather than another for a particular pupil will not be finally determined at the age of 11, but will be subject to review as the child's special gifts and capacities develop. At the age of 13, or even later, there will be facilities for transfer to a different type of education, if the original one proves to have been unsuitable....

28. If this choice is to be a real one, it is manifest that conditions in the different types of secondary schools must be broadly equivalent. Under present conditions the secondary school enjoys a prestige in the eyes of parents and the general public which completely overshadows all other types of school for children over 11. Inheriting as it does a distinguished tradition from the old English Grammar School it offers the advantages of superior premises and staffing and a longer school life for its pupils.... An academic training is ill-suited for many of the pupils who find themselves moving along a narrow educational path bounded by the School Certificate and leading into a limited field of opportunity. Further, too many of the nation's abler children are attracted into a type of education which prepares primarily for the University and for the administrative and clerical professions; too few find their way into schools from which the design and craftsmanship sides of industry are recruited. If education is to serve the interests both of the child and of the

nation, some means must be found of correcting this bias and of directing ability into the field where it will find its realisation.

29. Compared with the grammar schools the senior schools have a recent history.... They offer a general education for life, closely related to the interests and environment of the pupils and of a wide range embracing the literary as well as the practical, e.g. agricultural sides....

30. Junior Technical Schools ... give a general education associated with preparation for entry to one or another of the main branches of industry or commerce[;] they have grown up in close relation to local needs and opportunities and employment....

31. Such then, will be the three main types of secondary schools to be known as grammar, modern and technical schools. It would be wrong to suppose that they will necessarily remain separate and apart. Different types may be combined in one building or on one site as considerations of convenience and efficiency may suggest. In any case the free interchange of pupils from one type of education to another must be facilitated....

36. There has been a very general wish, not confined to representatives of the Churches, that religious education should be given a more defined place in the life and work of the schools, springing from the desire to revive the spiritual and personal values in our society and in our national tradition....

37. In order to emphasise the importance of the subject provision will be made for the school day in all primary and secondary schools to begin with a corporate act of worship, except where this is impracticable owing to the nature of the school premises, and for religious instruction to be given. At present this is the practice in the great majority of schools and this practice will receive statutory sanction and be universal.

Educational Reconstruction, Cmd 6458, London, 1943, pp. 3–4, 7, 9, 10–11.

11.4 Public reaction to proposed reform

Public interest in educational reform tended to focus on the question of whether it would mean equal educational opportunity for children from all classes.

The Education White Paper
The increasing interest in education, and approval for the proposals outlined in the White Paper are again reported.

In mining and quarry districts it is said that education has been popularly discussed in quarry cabins and pubs for the first time. People are asking: 'Will it really mean that my son will have the same chance as the Works Manager's son?'

The proposal to raise the school leaving age seems to be the point most often discussed. Most people are said to be in favour of this, many favouring 'education till 16 and over, with part-time continuation to the age of 18'; but a few suggest that 'some children do not benefit from the education given, and would be better apprenticed earlier to suitable trades'. A small minority fear that we may become too educated and wonder 'who will do the labourers' jobs'.

Other points approved are the proposals to introduce more nursery schools ... to abolish examinations at 11, and 'the attempt to solve the system of dual control'....

A minority are critical, mainly on the grounds that 'half the new ideas are impractical and too expensive'. Teachers in particular are said to consider the proposals 'handsome on paper, but unlikely to make any real changes in the present position.'

'The education white paper', Home Intelligence report, 29 July 1943, INF 1/292, Public Record Office, London.

11.5   Norwood Report

The Norwood Report on secondary education provided the official basis for claiming there should be three types of education to provide for the presumed three types of students.

... the terms of our reference immediately suggest as a first question:– 'If the curriculum necessarily contributes to the achieving of the purpose of secondary education, what is that purpose?'...

We believe that education cannot stop short of recognising the ideals of truth and beauty and goodness as final and binding for all times and in all places, as ultimate values; we do not believe that these ideals are of temporary convenience only, as devices for holding together society till they can be dispensed with as knowledge grows and organisation becomes more scientific. Further, we hold that the recognition of such values implies, for most people at least, a religious interpretation of life which for us must mean the Christian interpretation of life. We have no sympathy, therefore, with a theory of education which pre-supposes that its aim can be dictated by the provisional findings of special Sciences, whether biological, psychological or socio-logical, that the function of education is to fit pupils to determine their outlook and conduct according to the changing needs and the changing standards of the day....

The evolution of education has in fact thrown up certain groups, each of which can and must be treated in a way appropriate to itself. Whether such groupings are distinct on strictly psychological grounds, whether they represent types of mind, whether the differences are differences in kind or in degree, these are questions which it is not necessary to pursue....

For example, English education has in practice recognised the pupil who is interested in learning for its own sake, who can grasp an argument or follow a piece of connected reasoning.... Such pupils, educated by the curriculum commonly associated with the Grammar School, have entered the learned professions or have taken up higher administrative or business posts....

Again, the history of technical education has demonstrated the importance of recognising the needs of the pupil whose interests and abilities lie markedly in the field of applied science or applied art.... The various kinds of technical school were not instituted to satisfy the intellectual needs of an arbitrarily assumed group of children, but to prepare boys and girls for taking up certain crafts – engineering, agriculture and the like....

Again, there has of late years been recognition, expressed in the framing of curricula and otherwise, of still another grouping of pupils, and another grouping of occupations. The pupil in this group deals more easily with concrete things than with ideas. He may have much ability, but it will be in the realm of facts....

The time has come, we believe, when the real meaning of secondary education, the significance of child-centred education, the value of the Grammar School tradition, the difficulties of the present Secondary Schools should all be recognised and admitted. This means that within a framework of secondary education the needs of the three broad groups of pupils which we discussed earlier should be met within three broad types of secondary education, each type containing the possibility of variation and each school offering alternative courses which would yet keep the school true to type. Accordingly we would advocate that there should be three types of education, which we think of as the secondary Grammar, the secondary Technical, the secondary Modern, that each type should have such parity as amenities and conditions can bestow; parity of esteem in our view cannot be conferred by administrative decree nor by equality of cost per pupil; it can only be won by the school itself....

Hitherto we have spoken of secondary Grammar Schools, Technical Schools and Modern Schools. We have urged that in amenities, buildings, playing fields and staffing ratio they should enjoy similar conditions. It is appropriate at this point to consider whether they should occupy separate buildings or whether there are circumstances which permit of one type of school being combined with another in the same building and under the control of one Head Master or Mistress.

The phrase 'multilateral school' has frequently been used in the evidence offered to us orally and in writing. It is a phrase which few of our witnesses have used in the same sense.... The vagueness of the phrase has in our opinion been responsible for much confusion of thought and statement, and in the interest of clarity we propose to avoid it, even at the risk of using a clumsy nomenclature....

The question now arises whether types of school could be combined under one roof and in one direction, so as to make a 'two-type' or 'three-type' school.... Apart however from the Technical School, a two-type school combining Grammar School and Modern School seems to be satisfactory in certain circumstances.... On the other hand the tradition of English education has always valued human contacts and is not favourable to large schools in which the Head Master cannot have sufficient knowledge of each boy; thus a maximum figure is imposed beyond which expansion is undesirable, and in this connexion it must always be remembered that there are far more pupils for whom a Grammar School is appropriate....

The grounds for including Domestic Subjects in the curriculum are variously stated in the evidence submitted to us: briefly, they

are, first, that knowledge of such subjects is a necessary equipment for all girls as potential makers of homes.... It is assumed
that the majority of girls do not receive at home training
sufficient to turn them into good makers of homes. If this is true –
and we cannot disprove it – then the opportunity of some
minimum course of training at school is a necessity for all girls as
girls and the training at school must necessarily take nothing or
little for granted and must start from the beginning....

Accordingly we take the view that every girl before she leaves
school should have had the opportunity to take a minimum
course which would give her the essential elements of Needle-
work, Cookery and Laundrywork.... For many girls much more
than the minimum course is clearly desirable....

Curriculum and Examinations in Secondary Schools (Norwood Report),
London, 1943, pp. viii, 2–3, 14, 18–19, 127–8.

11.6   Fees in secondary schools?

> Educational reformers such as R. H. Tawney were con-
> cerned that by requiring fees in direct-grant schools the
> Education Bill would perpetuate class divisions rather than
> undermine them.

When you have given us so much it seems ungracious to press for
more. But I am seriously troubled by one point. It is the apparent
intention of the Bill to retain fees in secondary schools other than
maintained schools. The educational arguments in favour of
abolishing fees in all secondary schools receiving public money
are now widely accepted. They have not, as far as I know, been
answered; and they have recently been endorsed by a majority of
the Fleming Committee containing four or five headmasters and
headmistresses on it. The retention of fees in Direct Grant
Schools will perpetuate a division within secondary education
based not on educational, but on social grounds, and will do so at
the very moment, when, thanks to you, other such divisions are
being at last cleared away, and when public opinion, as a whole,
is prepared to see all of them go. It will really be a tragedy if this
particular mill-stone is to be tied around our necks for the next
quarter of a century....

Is it too late to reconsider the policy of the Bill on the point in question?

R. H. Tawney to R. A. Butler, 21 December 1943, Conservative Party Archive RAB 2/3, f. 12, Bodleian Library, Oxford.

11.7   Opinion on the Education Bill

> The reform proposals were resented by Catholics and revived prewar religious animosity.

During the past four weeks widespread approval has much outweighed criticism, though interest is apparently much greater among the teaching profession and 'progressive' people than with the general public.

There is, however, some fear that the Bill will not be put into operation within a reasonable time; the chief reason for doubt being fear that the shortage of teachers will make much of the Bill impractical. Moreover, a number think conditions, particularly pay, must be improved if the problem of recruitment is ever to be solved.

Criticism comes largely from the following:

(a) *Roman Catholics* (Six Regions), who are said to be in a 'militant temper' about the financial proposals and to fear that unless some further alleviation is granted they will be unable to meet the necessary expenses of rebuilding, etc.; it is said, also, that they object to the 'Fascist doctrine' of teachers receiving their ideas from the County Council or Board of Education.

Non-Catholics are reported to be annoyed with the Roman Catholics' 'uncompromising' attitude and to hope that no concessions will be granted them (Six Regions).

(b) *Lower income groups*, especially in rural areas, who object to the raising of the school leaving age (Six Regions). 'Children at fourteen should stop learning and start earning.'

'The Education Bill', Home Intelligence weekly report, 3 February 1944, INF 1/292, Public Record Office, London.

11.8   Equal pay for women teachers?

In March 1944 the House of Commons passed an amendment to the Education Bill forbidding sex differentiation in
pay scales. The Cabinet refused to accept that reform and
secured its defeat by insisting on a second vote and treating
it as a vote of confidence in the government.

The President of the Board of Education explained that Clause 82
had been included in the Bill to meet the views of the teachers.
The Clause enabled the Minister to secure that the remuneration
paid to teachers was in accordance with the scales recommended
by the Burnham Committees – independent bodies representing
both teachers and local authorities. The result of the amendment
carried against the Government was to put the Minister in a
position in which he had to interfere with the proceedings of the
Burnham Committees to the extent of requiring them to fix scales
applicable equally to men and women. Both he and his prede-
cessors had always avoided any interference with the proceedings
of the Burnham Committees, on the ground that bodies of this
kind must have complete freedom to reach their own decisions....
    The Minister of Labour and National Service agreed that the
question must be treated as a major issue of confidence. Any sign
of weakness on the part of the Government would have the worst
possible effect on industrial relations. He agreed with the
President of the Board of Education that it would be disastrous to
depart from the principle of non-interference with the decision of
independent tribunals on wage questions.

War Cabinet minute, 28 March 1944, CAB 65/41, WM (44) 42, Public
Record Office, London.

11.9   Public opinion on equal pay

Public opinion supported equal pay, even though some
women opposed it on the ground that it might reduce
employment opportunities for females.

Equal pay and the Education Bill
The debate on clause 82 of the Education Bill has stimulated
widespread discussion of the question of equal pay. Many people

are glad to know the subject is to be raised again, and think it calls for a full debate. Though opinion is divided, support for the principle of equal pay appears to outweigh opposition. Objections are based on the fear that it might mean either smaller salaries for men or, alternatively, less chance of a job for women.

'Equal pay and the Education Bill', Home Intelligence report, 6 April 1944, INF 1/292, Public Record Office, London.

11.10 Percy Report on technological education

Before the war, Lord Percy had warned that British economic growth was being held back by inadequate opportunities for higher technological education. Although the war strengthened support for that view, the reforms proposed in the Percy Report were not implemented in the immediate postwar period. It thus provides another example of a missed opportunity for reform.

2. The evidence submitted to us concurs in the general view: first, that the position of Great Britain as a leading industrial nation is being endangered by a failure to secure the fullest possible application of science to industry; and second that this failure is partly due to deficiencies in education. The annual intake into the industries of the country of men trained by Universities and Technical Colleges has been, and still is, insufficient both in quantity and quality.... In particular, the experience of war has shown that the greatest deficiency in British industry is the shortage of scientists and technologists who can also administer and organise, and can apply the results of research to development....

4. In any effective programme of action on these lines, it will be essential to distinguish between the functions of Universities and Technical Colleges.... Industry must look mainly to Universities for the training of scientists, both for research and development, and of teachers of science; it must look mainly to Technical Colleges for technical assistants and craftsmen....

6. We shall attempt in this Report to suggest an organisation of higher technological education which will be more responsive and adaptable to the needs of industry....

29. We recommend, therefore, the selection of a strictly limited number of Technical Colleges in which there should be developed technological courses of a standard comparable with that of University degree courses.

Ministry of Education, *Higher Technological Education* (Report of the Special Committee on Higher Technological Education, chaired by Lord Percy), London, 1945, pp. 5–6, 11.

12

Employment policy

The white paper on employment policy has been portrayed as a dramatic shift in government policy, reflecting a wartime acceptance of Keynesian theories by both major parties. The following documents, however, reveal fundamental differences over employment policy which were not resolved during the war and which may account for the inconsistencies between different sections of the white paper. Conservative doubts about the economic controls associated with a full-employment policy were reinforced by F. A. Hayek's *The Road to Serfdom*. The 1947 Industrial Charter is now considered by some historians to be the point at which the Conservative Party accepted a full-employment policy using Keynesian deficit spending to minimise unemployment.[1]

12.1 Postwar problems: employment

Despite the intense public debate on the Beveridge Report, opinion surveys indicated the public was most concerned about postwar employment and housing.

The post-war problems which receive the most attention are:

(a) *Employment:* Anxiety about the prospects of post-war employment are widely reported among working-class people, particularly from areas which suffered a high rate of unemployment in prewar years. There are widespread fears of heavy unemployment after the war – 'It will be just the same as last time, only worse for getting jobs' – and the position of the men in

---

[1] Rodney Lowe, 'The Second World War, consensus, and the foundation of the welfare state', *Twentieth Century British History*, 1, 2, 1990, p. 160.

the Forces and their absorption into industry continues to be anxiously discussed.

'Postwar problems', Home Intelligence report, 22 July 1943, INF 1/92, Public Record Office, London.

12.2 Persuading the Prime Minister

> In briefing Churchill on the white paper on employment policy, Lord Cherwell, Paymaster General and one of Churchill's closest personal advisers, shrewdly portrayed it as a compromise between fiscal conservatives and Keynesians that fulfilled Churchill's earlier pledge to provide work.

This White Paper endeavours to fulfil your promise of Work.

The White Paper sets out a large number of proposals, the principal of which are listed in Lord Woolton's minute. Most of them, I think, are very good....

Chapters III, IV, V, VI contain proposals for mandatory steady employment in the long run. These of course are the most important, since upon their success the solvency of all social insurance schemes etc. must depend. Although there are a host of consequential proposals the Government policy set forth depends on two main features:

(1) For many years economists have been agreed that the well-known snowball effect by which unemployment creates unemployment could be overcome if purchasing power in the country could be maintained....

The Committee[2] agreed unanimously that in broad outline this could and should be done by various means. The Government and local authorities should accelerate public works programmes; public utilities should be encouraged to put in hand extension or renewal projects; capital industries should be persuaded to switch production to the types of article needed for public investment and standing high on the reserve list of public works. Again, consuming power should be maintained; in the first instance by temporary reduction in the social insurance contributions when a

---

[2] War Reconstruction Committee, chaired by Lord Woolton, Minister of Reconstruction.

slump threatens; to this might be added, if necessary, some form of variation in taxation such as the use of deferred credits which could be paid out and put into circulation when unemployment increased.

The acceptance of this principle is a most significant innovation and I think one of the most important steps that has ever been taken in dealing with the unemployment problem.

(2) Connected with this policy is the principle of trying to secure so far as possible a balanced industry in the various parts of the country....

To a certain extent of course the White Paper represents a compromise, but I think it is a very satisfactory one. At the very last moment certain voices were raised against the Treasury scheme of deferred credits (mentioned in para. 72), it being suggested that these might be paid out at crucial moments as an electoral manoeuvre. I think this is a misapprehension. It is intended that the disbursements should be automatically linked to the state of the unemployment market so that they would be entirely immune from the risk of log-rolling. I am most anxious that this possibility of varying taxation, which after all is only adumbrated, should not be left out, since the other measures as they stand would not be enough to counter the variations of unemployment with which we have been faced heretofore. It is true that these other measures we propose should reduce the size of the problem – perhaps even so much that we shall not need to introduce this particular countermeasure. But it is essential it should be mentioned as a possibility in reserve lest we are faced with the criticism that we are merely providing a palliative.

Lord Cherwell to Prime Minister, 17 May 1944, PREM 4/96/6, Public Record Office, London.

12.3   Cabinet discussion of the white paper

There were sharp clashes over what to include in the *Employment Policy* white paper when the Reconstruction Committee drafted it; these divisions continued when it reached the War Cabinet. Labour ministers sought a commitment to maintaining full employment through demand management. Conservative ministers preferred limiting the objective to a high level of employment and were reluctant to grant the government powers to establish an effective system of demand management.

(a) Reference was made to the proposal in paragraph 72 of the White Paper that rates of taxation should be varied for the purpose of maintaining employment. Some Ministers on the Reconstruction Committee had been impressed by the political dangers which this method involved, and would have preferred that the Paper include no reference to it.

The War Cabinet decided that the suggestion should stand, in the form embodied in paragraph 72....

(c) The Lord Privy Seal [Lord Beaverbrook] said that, while otherwise in full agreement with the proposals in the Paper, he thought that the suggestions for stimulating private capital investment during times of depression did not go far enough. The reluctance to embark on private capital expenditure at such times would not, he thought, be overcome by variations of interest rates. He would like to see this part of the scheme strengthened by the addition of some method which would offer greater inducements to undertake capital expenditure at the onset of a depression, with a view to evening out the fluctuations in private investment.

War Cabinet minute, 19 May 1944, CAB 65/42, Public Record Office, London.

12.4 The *Employment Policy* white paper

Although the white paper has been portrayed as an example of coalition consensus, it contains ample evidence of the tension between the coalition parties. Paragraphs 74 and 77 seem especially inconsistent, reflecting the continuing disagreement within the government.

The Government accept as one of their primary aims and responsibilities the maintenance of a high and stable level of employment after the war. This Paper outlines the policy which they propose to follow in pursuit of that aim....

A country will not suffer from mass unemployment so long as the total demand for its goods and services is maintained at a high level. But in this country we are obliged to consider external no less than internal demand....

If ... the necessary expansion of our external trade can be assured, the Government believe that widespread unemployment in this country can be prevented by a policy for maintaining total internal expenditure.

... employment cannot be created by Act of Parliament or by Government action alone ... the success of the policy outlined in this Paper will ultimately depend on ... the efforts of employers and workers in industry; for without a rising standard of industrial efficiency we cannot achieve a high level of employment combined with a rising standard of living.

41. The Government are prepared to accept in future the responsibility for taking action at the earliest possible stage to arrest a threatened slump. This involves a new approach and a new responsibility for the State....

62. Public investment can, however, be used more directly as an instrument of employment policy.

Only a small proportion of public capital expenditure is undertaken by the central Government, by far the greater part being within the province of local authorities and public utility undertakings. In the past, capital expenditure by these authorities has generally followed the same trend as private capital expenditure – it has fallen in times of slump and risen in times of boom, and has tended therefore to accentuate the peaks and depressions of the trade cycle. In the future, Government policy will be directed to correcting this sympathetic movement ... for the purpose of maintaining general employment it is desirable that public investment should actually expand when private investment is declining and should contract in periods of boom. There are, however, practical limits to the extent to which Government action can produce swings in public investment to offset such swings in private investment as it cannot prevent. Thus, a large part of the capital expenditure of public authorities – for example on housing, schools, and hospitals – is dictated by urgent public needs, the satisfaction of which cannot readily be postponed to serve the purposes of employment policy. And in the other direction, the Government could not compel substantial acceleration of the capital programmes of these public authorities without much more power of direction than they now possess. There are, therefore, limits to the policy; but within those limits the Government believe that they can influence public capital expenditure to an extent which will be of material value for the purpose of maintaining employment....

66. The Government believe that in the past the power of public expenditure, skilfully applied, to check the onset of a depression has been underestimated. The whole notion of pressing forward quickly with public expenditure when incomes were falling and the outlook was dark has, naturally enough, encountered strong resistance from persons who are accustomed, with good reason, to conduct their private affairs according to the very opposite principle. Such resistance can, however, be overcome if public opinion is brought to the view that periods of trade recession provide an opportunity to improve the permanent equipment of society by the provision of better housing, public buildings, means of communication, power and water supplies, etc....

74. None of the main proposals contained in this Paper involves deliberate planning for a deficit in the National Budget in years of sub-normal trade activity. A policy of low interest rates is helpful rather than otherwise to the Budget. Any action which can be taken to improve our foreign balance works in the same direction. The designed variations in the capital position of the social insurance fund will not affect the Revenue Budget. Financial inducements to public authorities to expand capital expenditure will mainly take the form of an annual grant towards meeting recurrent charges on the loans raised and their burden will consequently be spread over a long period. Moreover, the success of measures designed to stabilise the national income and prevent cyclical depressions will have the effect of ironing out budget deficits which are normally associated with severe depression....

77. The policy of steadily decreasing the dead-weight debt, while other forms of debt are increasing, does not mean a rigid policy of balancing the Budget each year regardless of the state of trade. Such a policy is not required by statute nor is it part of our tradition. There is nothing to prevent the Chancellor of the Exchequer in the future, as in the past, from taking into account the requirements of trade and employment in framing his annual Budget. At the same time, to the extent that the policies proposed in this Paper affect the balancing of the Budget in a particular

year, they certainly do not contemplate any departure from the principle that the Budget must be balanced over a longer period.

Employment Policy, Parliamentary Papers 1943–44, vol. 8, Cmd 6527, pp. 3, 16, 21–2, 24–5.

12.5 The Labour Party and the white paper

Although the white paper on employment has been portrayed as an example of the wartime policy consensus, the Labour Party objected to its specific proposals and endorsed only the principle of state intervention to maintain employment.

The Chairman referred to the three-days debate which was likely to take place next week on the Government's White Paper on Full Employment, and stated that although the exact wording of the Motion to be tabled by the Government was not yet known, the [Labour Party's] Administrative Committee were of the opinion that, provided it did not pledge the Party to support the particular proposals contained in the White Paper but only the general question of the assumption by the Government of responsibility for the maintenance of employment after the war, it should be supported.... This recommendation was APPROVED.

Parliamentary Labour Party minute, 14 June 1944, archives of the Parliamentary Labour Party, London (Harvester Press, microfiche).

12.6 Fear of postwar unemployment

During the war's final year the reduction in employment in war factories fuelled fears that peace would bring a return to prewar unemployment levels. The perception that employers' attitude toward workers was hardening may have contributed to the increasing sense of class tension in the war's final months, as also noted in document 2.15.

Fear of unemployment (All Regions) in the immediate and the postwar future is causing widespread uneasiness – especially among industrial workers – and a good deal of unrest. Some, however, think it should be possible to find jobs for everybody – to meet the demand 'for the peacetime goods of which the world has been starved'; and some, too, have been encouraged by the White Paper on the re-allocation of man-power between the armed forces and civilian employment.

Nevertheless, fear of unemployment far outweighs hope; it is attributed to the following factors:

(a) *The present position in industry* (All Regions). Particular mention is made of:

(i)   Redundancy and/or enforced idleness in war factories (Nine Regions); 'Hundreds of men and women turn up at the factories every day and have nothing to do'....

(viii) Hardening attitude of employers in industries affected by redundancy (Two Regions); 'they are trying to break workers down for post-war exploitation.... Gone are the days of co-operation and any deference to labour; once more labour is a commodity to be bought at the cheapest price'. Workers also allege that employers are using redundancy and the cancellation of [military] deferment as a means of getting rid of awkward employees.

'Employment – present and postwar', Home Intelligence report, 7 December 1944, INF 1/292, Public Record Office, London.

12.7   Economic planning and totalitarianism

Hayek's *The Road to Serfdom* was the most influential wartime critique of the trend toward collectivism. His claim that using economic planning and controls to maintain full employment would lead to a totalitarian state was welcomed by several prominent Conservatives.

The question raised by economic planning is, therefore, not merely whether we shall be able to satisfy what we regard as our more or less important needs in the way we prefer. It is whether it shall be we who decide what is more, and what is less, important for us, or whether this is to be decided by the planner....

The authority directing all economic activity would control not merely the part of our lives which is concerned with inferior things; it would control the allocation of the limited means for all our ends. And whoever controls all economic activity must therefore decide which are to be satisfied and which not. This is really the crux of the matter.... Since under modern conditions we are for almost everything dependent on means which our fellow-men provide, economic planning would involve direction of almost the whole of our life....

That no single purpose must be allowed in peace to have absolute preference over all others applies even to the one aim which everybody now agrees comes in the front rank: the conquest of unemployment. There can be no doubt that this must be the goal of our greatest endeavor; even so, it does not mean that such an aim should be allowed to dominate us to the exclusion of everything else, that, as the glib phrase runs, it must be accomplished 'at any price'. It is, in fact, in this field that the fascination of vague but popular phrases like 'full employment' may well lead to extremely shortsighted measures....

There will always be a possible maximum of employment in the short run which can be achieved by giving all people employment where they happen to be and which can be achieved by monetary expansion. But not only can this maximum be maintained solely by progressive inflationary expansion and with the effect of holding up those redistributions of labor between industries made necessary by the changed circumstances ...: to aim always at the maximum of employment achievable by monetary means is a policy which is certain in the end to defeat its own purposes.

Friedrich A. Hayek, *The Road to Serfdom*, Chicago, 1944, pp. 91–2, 206, 208.

12.8 Churchill and economic planning

Churchill used his first election broadcast to attack collectivism and the economic controls Beveridge and others thought necessary to maintain full employment. His claim that the powerful state urged by the Labour Party would lead to totalitarianism suggests Hayek's influence.

My friends, I must tell you that a Socialist policy is abhorrent to the British ideas of freedom.... There can be no doubt that

Socialism is inseparably interwoven with totalitarianism and the abject worship of the State. It is not alone that property in all its forms is struck at, but that liberty in all its forms is challenged by the fundamental conceptions of Socialism. Look how, even today, they hunger for controls of every kind, as if these were delectable foods instead of war-time inflictions and monstrosities. There is to be one State to which all are to be obedient.... This State is to be the arch-employer, the arch-planner, the arch-administrator and ruler.... How is an ordinary citizen or subject of the King to stand up against this formidable machine, which once it is in power will prescribe for every one of them where they are to work, what they are to work at, where they may go, and what they may say....

Here in old England ... we do not like to be regimented and ordered about and have every action of our lives prescribed for us. In fact we punish criminals by sending them to Wormwood Scrubs and Dartmoor where they get full employment.

Winston Churchill's election broadcast of 4 June 1945, *The Listener,* 7 June 1945, p. 629.

Guide to further reading

General

Angus Calder's *The People's War: Britain 1939–1945*, London, 1969, remains the best general survey of the wartime home front. Calder's *The Myth of the Blitz*, London, 1991, suggests how the mythology relating to the Blitz emerged and why it has become such an integral part of national ideology. Jose Harris provides an excellent guide to the debate on wartime social history in 'War and social history: Britain and the home front during the Second World War', *Contemporary European History*, 1, 1, 1992. Rodney Lowe reviews the historiography on the wartime origins of the welfare state from a different perspective in 'The Second World War, consensus, and the foundation of the welfare state', in *Twentieth Century British History*, 1, 2, 1990. Stephen Brooke questions the belief in consensus in *Labour's War: The Labour Party during the Second World War*, Oxford, 1992. Richard Cockett provides a useful guide to anti-collectivist sentiment in the wartime Conservative Party in *Thinking the Unthinkable: Think-Tanks and the Economic Counter-Revolution 1931–1983*, London, 1994. Harold L. Smith (ed.), *War and Social Change: British Society in the Second World War*, Manchester, 1986, contains chapters on wartime social structure and social policy.

Population and health

Several works by Jay Winter are especially useful: 'The demographic consequences of the war', in Smith, *War and Social Change*; 'Unemployment, nutrition and infant mortality in Britain, 1920–50', in Jay Winter (ed.), *The Working Class in*

Modern British History, Cambridge, 1983; and 'War, family, and fertility in twentieth-century Europe', in John R. Gillis, Louise A. Tilly, and David Levine (eds), *The European Experience of Declining Fertility, 1850–1970*, Oxford, 1992. Richard A. Soloway places the formation of the Royal Commission on Population in context in *Demography and Degeneration: Eugenics and the Declining Birthrate in Twentieth-Century Britain*, Chapel Hill, 1990. Pat Thane draws attention to the prewar origins of wartime demographic concerns in 'The debate on the declining birth rate in Britain: the "menace" of an ageing population, 1920s–1950s', *Continuity and Change*, 5, 1990. Cate Haste reviews wartime policy toward venereal disease and other sexual issues in *Rules of Desire. Sex in Britain: World War I to the Present*, London, 1992. Helen Jones provides a brief guide to wartime health issues in *Health and Society in Twentieth-Century Britain*, London, 1994.

Class

Penny Summerfield challenges the traditional view that the war substantially narrowed class differentials in 'The "leveling of class"', in Smith, *War and Social Change*. On the failure of wartime reforms to eliminate poverty see David Vincent, *Poor Citizens: The State and the Poor in Twentieth-Century Britain*, London, 1991. Tony Lane, *The Merchant Seamen's War*, Manchester, 1990, is an important example of the studies of specific groups of workers which demonstrate the continued importance of class conflict during the war. The interviews presented in Pete Grafton (ed.), *You, You and You! The People Out of Step with World War II*, London, 1981, draw attention to the continued importance of class in how people experienced the war.

Race and ethnicity

Colin Holmes, *John Bull's Island: Immigration and British Society, 1871–1971*, London, 1988, is a good overview. Tony Kushner provides the best study of anti-Semitism in *The*

Persistence of Prejudice: Antisemitism in British Society during the Second World War, Manchester, 1989. Kenneth Lunn, '"Good for a few hundreds at least": Irish labour recruitment into Britain during the Second World War', in Institute of Irish Studies, *Conference Proceedings in Irish Studies*, 1, 1993, is helpful on the Irish in Britain. On blacks and race relations see: Graham Smith, *When Jim Crow Met John Bull: Black American Soldiers in World War II Britain*, London, 1987; Ben Bousquet and Colin Douglas, *West Indian Women at War*, London, 1991; and David Reynolds, *Rich Relations: The American Occupation of Britain, 1942–1945*, London, 1995.

Women

The best survey is Gail Braybon and Penny Summerfield, *Out of the Cage: Women's Experiences in Two World Wars*, London, 1987. On women's reform movements see Harold L. Smith 'The womanpower problem in Britain during the Second World War', *Historical Journal*, 27, 4, 1984, and 'The problem of "equal pay for equal work" in Great Britain during World War II', *Journal of Modern History*, 53, 4, 1981. Dorothy Sheridan's 'Ambivalent memories: women and the 1939–45 war in Britain', *Oral History*, 18, 1, 1990, is helpful on women in the military. Wartime women's views are presented in Dorothy Sheridan (ed.), *Wartime Women: An Anthology of Women's Wartime Writing for Mass-Observation 1937–45*, London, 1990. Joyce Storey's autobiographical account, *Joyce's War 1939–1945*, London, 1992, describes a married woman's life during the war.

The family

Geoffery Field's article, 'Perspectives on the working-class family in wartime Britain, 1939–1945', *International Labor and Working-Class History*, 38, 1990, is the best starting point. Studies of evacuation, such as Travis L. Crosby, *The Impact of Civilian Evacuation in the Second World War*, London, 1986, and John Macnicol, 'The effect of the evacuation of schoolchildren on official attitudes to State intervention', in Smith, *War and Social*

Change, are very helpful. On children see Harry Hendrick, *Child Welfare: England 1872–1989*, London, 1994. Wartime children describe their experience of the war in Ben Wicks (ed.), *No Time to Wave Goodbye*, London, 1988. Wartime attitudes toward women and family are examined by Denise Riley, *The War in the Nursery: Theories of the Child and Mother*, London, 1983.

Crime

Edward Smithies provides the best general account in *Crime in Wartime: A Social History of Crime in World War II*, London, 1982. Wartime juvenile delinquency is carefully examined by Victor Bailey in *Delinquency and Citizenship: Reclaiming the Young Offender, 1914–1948*, Oxford, 1987.

Public opinion

Neil Stammers, *Civil Liberties in Britain During the Second World War*, London, 1984, reviews government attempts to control opinion. Ian McLaine's *Ministry of Morale: Home Front Morale and the Ministry of Information in World War II*, London, 1979, is essential. Steven Fielding, Peter Thompson and Nick Tiratsoo examine grassroots political opinion in *England Arise! The Labour Party and Popular Politics in the 1940s*, Manchester, 1995. Angus Calder and Dorothy Sheridan present a selection of contemporary opinion in *Speak for Yourself: A Mass-Observation Anthology, 1937–49*, London, 1984. For wartime Gallup poll results see George H. Gallup (ed.), *The Gallup International Public Opinion Polls: Great Britain 1937–1975. Vol. I 1937–1964*, New York, 1976.

Urban and rural society

Joanna Mack and Steve Humphries make good use of oral history in *The Making of Modern London 1939–1945: London at War*, London, 1985. On Coventry see Tony Mason, 'Looking back on the blitz', in Bill Lancaster and Tony Mason (eds), *Life and*

Labour in a Twentieth Century City: The Experience of Coventry, Coventry, 1986. John Stevenson examines the failure of the wartime planning movement to take root in 'Planner's moon? The Second World War and the planning movement', in Smith, *War and Social Change*. Andrew Cox, *Adversary Politics and Land: The Conflict Over Land and Property Policy in Post-War Britain*, Cambridge, 1984, and Junichi Hasegawa, *Replanning the Blitzed City Centre: A Comparative Study of Bristol, Coventry and Southampton 1941–50*, Buckingham, 1992, are useful guides to the conflict over town and country planning. On wartime rural life see Sadie Ward, *War in the Countryside 1939–45*, London, 1988.

Social insurance

Paul Addison, *The Road to 1945*, London, 1977, and Kevin Jefferys, *The Churchill Coalition and Wartime Politics, 1940–1945*, Manchester, 1991, review the debate on social policy from different perspectives. Rodney Lowe, *The Welfare State in Britain since 1945*, London, 1993, provides an important reassessment of wartime policy. John Hills, *et al.* (eds), *Beveridge and Social Security: an International Retrospective*, Oxford, 1994, is especially important on the Beveridge Report. The Beveridge Report's implications for single mothers are examined by Sylvie Pierce, 'Single mothers and the concept of female dependency in the development of the welfare state in Britain', *Journal of Comparative Family Studies*, 11, 1, 1980.

Family allowances and the National Health Service

John Macnicol, *The Movement for Family Allowances 1918–1945*, London, 1981, remains the best study of that topic. Susan Pedersen draws attention to the gender implications of family allowances in *Family, Dependence, and the Origins of the Welfare State: Britain and France, 1914–1945*, Cambridge, 1993. On the wartime changes in health policy see Charles Webster, *Problems of Health Care: The National Health Service before 1957*, London, 1988.

Education

Although P. H. J. H. Gosden's *Education in the Second World War: A Study in Policy and Administration*, London, 1976, is a useful guide to the government's internal policy discussions, Brian Simon's *Education and the Social Order 1940–1990*, London, 1991, conveys the public debate especially well. Kevin Jefferys, 'R. A. Butler, the Board of Education and the 1944 Education Act', *History*, 69, 1984, Brian Simon, 'The 1944 Education Act: a Conservative measure?', *History of Education*, 15, 1986, and Deborah Thom, 'The 1944 Education Act: the "art of the possible"?', in Smith, *War and Social Change*, are helpful on the 1944 Education Act. Kevin Jefferys provides an important primary source in *Labour and the Wartime Coalition: From the Diary of James Chuter Ede 1941–45*, London, 1987.

Employment policy

On the debate as to whether the white paper on employment policy represented a commitment to Keynesian economic policy, see Jim Tomlinson, *Employment Policy*, Oxford, 1987, and Sean Glynn and Alan Booth (eds), *The Road to Full Employment*, London, 1987.

Index

187